From Code to Cloud

The Complete Journey of Cross-Platform Application Development Using Python, C#, and Modern DevOps Practices

THOMPSON CARTER

Table of Content

TABLE OF CONTENTS

Introduction

In today's fast-paced and interconnected digital world, the demand for applications that seamlessly run across multiple platforms is growing at an unprecedented rate. Whether you are developing for **mobile, desktop**, or the **web**, users expect consistent, high-quality experiences regardless of their device or operating system. Cross-platform development has emerged as a solution to this challenge, allowing developers to write applications that can run on multiple platforms with a single codebase, significantly reducing time and cost while improving the overall user experience.

This book, **"From Code to Cloud: The Complete Journey of Cross-Platform Application Development Using Python, C#, and Modern DevOps Practices,"** is designed to provide both new and experienced developers with the knowledge and tools to effectively navigate the complex world of cross-platform development. By leveraging the power of **Python, C#**, and modern **DevOps practices**, we will explore how to build scalable, high-performance, and maintainable applications that work seamlessly across a wide range of devices and platforms.

The development landscape is constantly evolving, with new tools, frameworks, and best practices emerging every day. Cross-platform development is no exception. Today, developers can rely on powerful frameworks like **Flutter**, **Xamarin**, and **React Native**, as well as cloud services like **AWS**, **Azure**, and **Google Cloud**, to build applications that run efficiently on multiple platforms, from **iOS** and **Android** to **Windows**, **macOS**, and **Linux**. By the end of this book, you will have a deep understanding of how to utilize these technologies to streamline your development process, reduce redundancy, and create apps that provide consistent and engaging experiences for users across all platforms.

But cross-platform development is not just about writing code that runs on multiple platforms; it's also about designing a robust and flexible infrastructure that can scale as your user base grows. This book will take you through the complete journey of building a cross-platform application, from the initial stages of **conceptualization** and **design** to the final steps of **deployment**, **monitoring**, and **maintenance**. You will learn not only the technical skills needed to develop for multiple platforms but also how to integrate modern **DevOps practices** to automate repetitive tasks, streamline collaboration, and ensure that your applications are always up to date and running at peak performance.

We will begin with a **fundamental understanding** of cross-platform development, introducing key principles, frameworks, and the languages that are the backbone of this approach—**Python** and **C#**. These languages, both popular in the development community, provide excellent cross-platform support and are backed by vibrant ecosystems and powerful libraries. We will delve into the details of tools like **Xamarin**, **Flutter**, and **React Native**, which allow you to write native-like apps that work across multiple platforms. You will also learn how to take advantage of the **cloud**, which plays a central role in modern application development, providing the infrastructure and services necessary to support millions of users across multiple regions.

Throughout this book, we will emphasize the importance of **performance**, **scalability**, and **user experience**—three critical pillars that make cross-platform applications successful. The focus will be on developing **efficient**, **reliable**, and **secure** applications that perform well even as user traffic grows exponentially. We will introduce key techniques for **optimizing performance, securing your**

7

app, and **automating deployments** to save time, reduce costs, and ensure smooth releases.

In addition to covering the technical aspects, this book will also provide you with **real-world examples** and **case studies** that demonstrate how to apply the concepts in actual development scenarios. From setting up **CI/CD pipelines** for automated testing and deployment, to integrating modern **monitoring tools** that ensure the health of your application post-launch, this book is a comprehensive guide to building robust cross-platform apps.

Whether you are a developer aiming to enhance your skills in cross-platform development or a project manager seeking to understand the latest best practices, this book is your go-to resource. By the time you finish this book, you will have gained valuable insights into not only how to write code that runs on multiple platforms, but also how to architect your apps for **global distribution**, **scale**, and **continuous improvement**.

The journey through **cross-platform development**, **DevOps automation**, and **cloud integration** can be complex, but with the right tools and knowledge, you can navigate this landscape efficiently and create high-quality applications that meet the demands of modern users. Let's dive in and start building apps that will succeed across platforms, regions, and cultures, delivering exceptional experiences to users worldwide.

CHAPTER 1

INTRODUCTION TO CROSS-PLATFORM DEVELOPMENT

Overview of Cross-Platform Development and Its Importance

Cross-platform development refers to the practice of building software applications that can run on multiple operating systems or platforms with minimal modifications. The key benefit of cross-platform development is the ability to create one codebase that works across a variety of devices and environments, saving time and resources in the development process. This approach is especially valuable in today's tech ecosystem, where users expect applications to work seamlessly across devices, from desktops to mobile phones and even smart devices.

In the past, developers had to write separate code for each platform (e.g., one for iOS, one for Android, one for Windows). Cross-platform frameworks and languages have revolutionized this approach, allowing developers to target multiple platforms without duplicating effort. This leads to faster development cycles, reduced maintenance costs, and a broader user reach.

Introduction to Python and C# as Powerful Languages for Cross-Platform Apps

Python and **C#** are two of the most popular programming languages in the development world today. They have distinct strengths and are both excellent choices for cross-platform development.

- **Python**: Known for its simplicity and readability, Python is highly favored for web applications, automation scripts, data science, and more. While it isn't traditionally used for mobile app development, frameworks like **Kivy**, **BeeWare**, and **PyQt** have made it possible to write cross-platform applications in Python. Python's flexibility and wide range of libraries make it a great choice for prototyping and building scalable applications quickly.

- **C#**: Developed by Microsoft, C# is a robust, object-oriented language widely used in desktop, web, and mobile app development. With the introduction of **Xamarin** and **.NET Core**, C# has become a key player in the cross-platform development space. Xamarin allows developers to write mobile apps that run on both iOS and Android from a single codebase, while .NET Core enables the creation of high-

11

performance, cross-platform applications for various operating systems like Windows, macOS, and Linux.

Both languages have strong communities, excellent documentation, and an array of libraries and tools that make them ideal choices for cross-platform development.

What DevOps Practices Bring to the Table for Modern Development

DevOps (Development and Operations) is a set of practices that combines software development (Dev) and IT operations (Ops) to shorten the development lifecycle and provide continuous delivery with high software quality. In the context of cross-platform development, DevOps practices bring several advantages:

- **Automation of Repetitive Tasks**: DevOps tools like **Jenkins**, **GitLab CI**, and **Travis CI** enable developers to automate testing, building, and deployment tasks. This is especially useful in cross-platform development, where code must be tested on various environments and devices. Automation reduces human error and increases the speed of delivery.

- **Continuous Integration and Continuous Delivery (CI/CD)**: CI/CD pipelines are essential in modern software development. They ensure that code changes are automatically tested, integrated, and deployed without manual intervention. For cross-platform apps, this means that developers can deploy updates across all platforms simultaneously, ensuring that all users benefit from the latest features and bug fixes.

- **Collaboration and Feedback Loops**: DevOps encourages collaboration between development and operations teams, allowing for faster communication and quicker resolution of issues. In cross-platform development, it ensures that platform-specific concerns are addressed early and that feedback is integrated into the development process.

- **Scalability and Monitoring**: DevOps practices also include monitoring applications in production to ensure they perform optimally. Tools like **Prometheus** and **Datadog** can be used to track the performance of cross-platform apps and ensure that they function well across different devices and environments.

By integrating DevOps practices into cross-platform development, teams can increase the reliability, scalability, and speed of their applications, ensuring that they meet the demands of modern users and stay competitive in the market.

This chapter sets the foundation for the entire journey of cross-platform development, introducing the key concepts and technologies that will be explored further throughout the book. From understanding why cross-platform development is so crucial in today's software landscape to the role of Python, C#, and DevOps in creating efficient, high-quality applications, this chapter lays the groundwork for developers at any skill level.

CHAPTER 2

FUNDAMENTALS OF PYTHON AND C#

Basic Syntax and Concepts in Python and C#

Python and **C#** are both versatile, high-level programming languages, but they have different syntax and design philosophies. Understanding their basic syntax and key concepts is crucial for writing efficient and maintainable cross-platform applications.

Python:

- **Syntax**: Python is known for its simplicity and readability. The language follows a clean, minimalistic design where code is easy to write and understand. Python uses indentation (rather than braces or parentheses) to define code blocks, which encourages readable code.
    - Example of a simple Python function:

    ```python
    python

    def greet(name):
    ```

```
print(f"Hello, {name}!")
greet("Alice")
```

- **Data Types**: Python is dynamically typed, meaning variables don't need to be declared with a type. The type is inferred during runtime. Common types include integers, floats, strings, lists, dictionaries, tuples, and sets.
  - o Example of variable assignment in Python:

    ```python
    name = "Alice"  # String
    age = 30  # Integer
    ```

- **Control Flow**: Python uses `if`, `elif`, and `else` for conditional branching, as well as `for` and `while` loops for iteration.
  - o Example of a loop in Python:

    ```python
    for i in range(5):
        print(i)
    ```

- **Object-Oriented Programming (OOP)**: Python supports OOP and allows you to define classes and objects.

o Example of a simple class in Python:

```python
class Car:
    def __init__(self, make, model):
        self.make = make
        self.model = model

    def display_info(self):
        print(f"Car:     {self.make} {self.model}")

car = Car("Toyota", "Camry")
car.display_info()
```

C#:

- **Syntax**: C# has a more structured syntax, relying on semicolons to end statements and curly braces to define code blocks. C# is statically typed, meaning variables must be declared with a type before they can be used.

  o Example of a simple C# function:

```csharp
using System;
```

17

```
class Program
{
    static void Greet(string name)
    {
        Console.WriteLine($"Hello,
{name}!");
    }

    static void Main()
    {
        Greet("Alice");
    }
}
```

- **Data Types**: C# has a range of built-in types, such as int, float, string, bool, char, and decimal, and all variables must be explicitly declared with their types.
  - o Example of variable declaration in C#:

```
csharp

string name = "Alice";
int age = 30;
```

- **Control Flow**: C# also uses if, else, and switch for conditional branching and for, foreach, while, and do-while loops for iteration.

18

- o Example of a loop in C#:

```csharp
for (int i = 0; i < 5; i++)
{
    Console.WriteLine(i);
}
```

- **Object-Oriented Programming (OOP)**: C# is a strongly object-oriented language and everything revolves around classes and objects. It supports inheritance, interfaces, and other OOP principles.
  - o Example of a simple class in C#:

```csharp
class Car
{
    public string Make { get; set; }
    public string Model { get; set;
}

    public void DisplayInfo()
    {
        Console.WriteLine($"Car:
{Make} {Model}");
    }
}
```

19

```
class Program
{
    static void Main()
    {
        Car car = new Car { Make =
"Toyota", Model = "Camry" };
        car.DisplayInfo();
    }
}
```

How Each Language Fits into the Cross-Platform Ecosystem

Python: Python is widely recognized for its flexibility and ease of use, especially in areas like scripting, web development, data science, and automation. Although it wasn't initially designed for mobile development, frameworks like **Kivy** and **BeeWare** have extended Python's reach to mobile devices and desktop platforms. Python is ideal for rapid prototyping and building applications that require extensive use of third-party libraries or web-based services. Python's rich ecosystem of packages makes it a go-to language for cross-platform apps that don't require complex, native UI interactions.

C#: C# is a strong contender in the cross-platform development space, particularly with the **Xamarin** framework, which allows developers to create native mobile apps for iOS and Android using a single C# codebase. Additionally, **.NET Core** (now **.NET 5+**) enables C# developers to create cross-platform applications that run on Windows, macOS, and Linux. Xamarin is particularly beneficial for mobile development, while .NET Core is used for cloud-based applications and APIs. C# shines in enterprise-level applications, game development (via **Unity**), and when building complex applications requiring solid performance.

Key Differences and Similarities Between Python and C#

Similarities:

1. **High-Level Languages**: Both Python and C# are high-level, object-oriented programming languages, meaning they abstract away many of the complexities of hardware management and memory handling.

2. **Garbage Collection**: Both languages automatically manage memory with garbage collection, which reduces the chances of memory leaks.

3. **Cross-Platform Capability**: Both languages support cross-platform development with the right frameworks (e.g., Kivy, Xamarin, .NET Core).

4. **Extensive Libraries**: Python and C# have vast ecosystems with numerous libraries and frameworks,

21

enabling rapid development in various domains such as web apps, mobile apps, and enterprise systems.

Differences:

1. **Typing System**: Python is dynamically typed, meaning that types are determined at runtime, while C# is statically typed, which means types must be defined at compile time. This makes C# a bit more structured but can also catch certain errors early in the development process.

2. **Syntax and Verbosity**: Python is often more concise and readable, whereas C# has a more verbose syntax, especially when it comes to defining classes, methods, and properties.

3. **Use Cases**: Python is heavily used in scientific computing, web development, and automation, while C# is more popular in desktop applications, mobile apps (via Xamarin), and game development (via Unity).

4. **Performance**: C# tends to perform better in resource-intensive applications because it is compiled to intermediate bytecode that runs on the **.NET runtime** (CLR). Python is interpreted, which can lead to slower execution times for certain tasks.

Conclusion

Understanding the fundamentals of Python and C# equips you with the knowledge to choose the right language for your cross-platform development needs. While Python's simplicity and rich ecosystem make it a great choice for rapid prototyping and web development, C#'s strong typing system, enterprise-level features, and powerful mobile development capabilities make it ideal for more complex applications. Both languages are capable of producing cross-platform applications, and your choice will depend on the specific requirements of your project.

CHAPTER 3

THE POWER OF CROSS-PLATFORM FRAMEWORKS

An Overview of Popular Cross-Platform Frameworks

Cross-platform frameworks are the backbone of modern application development, allowing developers to create applications that run on multiple platforms with minimal code modification. These frameworks abstract away the complexity of handling platform-specific issues, letting developers focus on building features rather than managing platform-specific details. Below are some popular frameworks used for Python and C# in cross-platform development.

1. Xamarin for C#

- **Overview**: Xamarin is a Microsoft-owned framework that allows developers to write mobile applications for both **iOS** and **Android** using a shared C# codebase. Xamarin utilizes a set of tools, including Xamarin.Forms (a UI toolkit), to ensure that apps look and behave like native apps on each platform.
- **Key Features**:

24

- o **Single Codebase**: Write one codebase in C# that runs on both Android and iOS.

- o **Native Performance**: Xamarin provides native performance because it compiles down to native code.

- o **Xamarin.Forms**: A UI toolkit that lets developers design cross-platform UIs with a single codebase.

- o **Access to Native APIs**: Xamarin allows access to native APIs and platform-specific features.

- o **Integration with .NET**: Xamarin works seamlessly with the .NET ecosystem, which provides a rich set of libraries for app development.

2. Kivy for Python

- **Overview**: Kivy is an open-source Python framework for building cross-platform applications, especially mobile applications. It supports Android, iOS, Linux, macOS, and Windows. Kivy focuses on providing a high level of flexibility and simplicity while allowing for rich UI designs.

- **Key Features**:
  - o **Multitouch Support**: Kivy was built with multitouch applications in mind, making it ideal for creating apps with advanced user interfaces.

o **Highly Customizable UI**: Kivy allows developers to design custom UIs using its own set of widgets, giving it flexibility for mobile and desktop applications.

o **Pythonic API**: The framework allows developers to write in Python, leveraging its simplicity and readability.

o **Cross-Platform**: Applications can be easily deployed on Android, iOS, Linux, Windows, and macOS.

o **Extensive Documentation**: Kivy comes with comprehensive documentation and examples for easy onboarding.

3. Flutter for Dart (although not directly related to Python or C#, it's a strong contender)

- **Overview**: Flutter is a Google-developed UI toolkit that enables developers to build natively compiled applications for mobile, web, and desktop from a single codebase using **Dart**. While Flutter is not directly related to Python or C#, its growing popularity in the cross-platform space warrants mention.

- **Key Features**:
    o **Single Codebase for Multiple Platforms**: Flutter allows you to write one codebase and

26

deploy on mobile (Android, iOS), web, and desktop (Linux, Windows, macOS).

- o **Hot Reload**: It enables developers to instantly see the results of code changes without rebuilding the app, improving development speed.
- o **Rich Widget Library**: Flutter offers a rich collection of customizable widgets for UI development.

4. React Native for JavaScript (briefly mentioned)

- **Overview**: React Native is a popular framework for building cross-platform mobile apps using **JavaScript**. It allows developers to write mobile apps for Android and iOS using the React paradigm, which is based on declarative UI components.
- **Key Features**:
  - o **Single Codebase**: A shared codebase for Android and iOS apps.
  - o **Native Modules**: React Native bridges the gap between JavaScript and native code for performance-critical features.
  - o **Fast Development**: Features like hot reloading speed up development and iteration times.

5. Qt for C++ and Python

27

- **Overview**: Qt is a widely-used framework for developing GUI applications that run across multiple platforms, including mobile and desktop. Qt can be used with **C++** or **Python** (via PyQt or PySide). It provides a wide range of features for GUI development and is highly optimized for performance.

- **Key Features**:
  - **Cross-Platform GUI**: Qt allows developers to write applications with sophisticated UIs that work on Windows, macOS, Linux, iOS, and Android.
  - **Performance**: Being a native framework, it offers excellent performance, especially for resource-intensive applications.
  - **Large Ecosystem**: Qt offers extensive libraries for handling everything from networking and databases to graphics and multimedia.

Real-World Examples of Frameworks in Action

1. Xamarin in Action: A Mobile Banking Application

- **Project Overview**: A bank needs to create a mobile application that works on both **Android** and **iOS** platforms. The challenge is to develop a native experience for both platforms while maintaining a single codebase.

- **How Xamarin Solves It**: Using Xamarin, the developers can write a single C# codebase that runs on both Android and iOS. Xamarin provides a **native performance** layer for the app, ensuring that the mobile banking app works efficiently on both platforms. The app can use **Xamarin.Forms** for shared UI components and platform-specific APIs when required for native features (such as secure transactions and camera access).

- **Outcome**: The app achieves a smooth and responsive UI across both platforms, with easy maintenance thanks to the shared codebase. Updates can be pushed simultaneously to both platforms.

2. Kivy in Action: A Fitness Tracker App

- **Project Overview**: A developer needs to build a cross-platform fitness tracker app that will run on **Android, iOS, Windows**, and **macOS**. The app needs to track fitness data, integrate with health APIs, and display custom graphs and analytics.

- **How Kivy Solves It**: Using Kivy, the developer writes the app in Python and takes advantage of Kivy's **multitouch support** to allow users to interact with the fitness data via touch gestures. The framework allows the app to have a **customizable UI** that looks consistent across platforms. Kivy's built-in support for handling

multimedia content makes it easy to show graphs and track metrics.

- **Outcome**: The fitness tracker app is successfully deployed across all platforms with the same codebase. The app is responsive, the touch interactions are smooth, and the code is easy to maintain.

3. Flutter for a Restaurant App

- **Project Overview**: A restaurant chain wants to develop a mobile app to allow customers to browse the menu, order food, and track delivery, with a seamless experience on both **Android** and **iOS**.
- **How Flutter Solves It**: The app is built using **Flutter**, leveraging its **rich set of widgets** to create an interactive and visually appealing UI. The **hot reload** feature speeds up the development process, allowing designers and developers to experiment with UI changes without long rebuilds.
- **Outcome**: The app is built quickly, with consistent design elements and smooth animations. The customer experience is identical across both platforms, reducing costs and time to market.

30

Conclusion

Cross-platform frameworks such as **Xamarin** for C# and **Kivy** for Python provide developers with powerful tools to build applications that work across multiple platforms without duplicating code. These frameworks enable faster development, easier maintenance, and better resource utilization. Whether you're creating a mobile banking app, a fitness tracker, or a restaurant app, these frameworks can help you deliver a high-quality, cross-platform experience. By leveraging the right tools for the job, developers can maximize productivity while providing end-users with a seamless experience across platforms.

CHAPTER 4

SETTING UP THE

DEVELOPMENT ENVIRONMENT

Setting up an efficient development environment is crucial to streamline your workflow and ensure that your applications are built smoothly, especially when developing cross-platform applications using Python and C#. In this chapter, we will go over how to set up a local development environment for both Python and C#, including essential tools like Integrated Development Environments (IDEs), version control systems, and other utilities to improve your productivity.

How to Set Up a Local Development Environment for Python and C#

Setting Up a Development Environment for Python

1. **Installing Python**
   - o First, you need to install **Python**. You can download it from the official Python website (python.org). The installation package is available for Windows, macOS, and Linux.

32

- o When installing on Windows, ensure that the box "Add Python to PATH" is checked during the installation process. This allows you to run Python from the command line directly.
- o On macOS and Linux, Python is often pre-installed. If needed, you can update Python using package managers like brew for macOS or apt for Linux.

2. **Installing Python Package Manager (pip)**
   - o Python uses **pip** to manage external libraries or packages. After installing Python, pip should automatically be installed.
   - o You can check if **pip** is installed by running the following command:

bash

```
python -m ensurepip --upgrade
```

   - o To install a package with pip, use:

bash

```
pip install package-name
```

3. **Setting Up a Virtual Environment**

- o A virtual environment isolates dependencies for different projects, preventing conflicts between packages. To create a virtual environment:

```bash

python -m venv myprojectenv
```

- o Activate the environment:
  - On Windows:

```bash

myprojectenv\Scripts\activate
```

  - On macOS/Linux:

```bash

source
myprojectenv/bin/activate
```

- o You can deactivate the environment anytime by running `deactivate`.

4. **Installing Essential Python Packages**
   - o There are various libraries available to enhance your development, such as:
     - **Flask/Django** for web applications
     - **Kivy** for mobile applications

- **NumPy/Pandas** for data manipulation
- **Requests** for making HTTP requests

o You can install these packages using pip:

```bash
pip install flask kivy numpy pandas
requests
```

Setting Up a Development Environment for C#

1. **Installing Visual Studio**

   o **Visual Studio** is the primary IDE for **C#** development. It supports .NET Core, Xamarin, and a variety of other tools needed for cross-platform development.

   o Download Visual Studio from the official website (Visual Studio Download) and follow the instructions to install the **Community Edition** (free) or any other suitable edition for your needs.

   o During installation, make sure to select the **.NET desktop development** and **Mobile development with .NET** workloads to ensure Xamarin and .NET Core tools are installed.

2. **Installing .NET SDK (Software Development Kit)**

   o To build cross-platform applications using **.NET Core**, download and install the **.NET SDK** from the official .NET website.

35

    o   After installing the SDK, you can verify it by typing:

```bash
```

```
dotnet --version
```

3. Creating a .NET Core Project

    o   Once Visual Studio and the .NET SDK are installed, you can create a new project directly from the Visual Studio IDE, or you can create a project from the command line using:

```bash
```

```
dotnet new console -n MyApp
cd MyApp
dotnet run
```

4. Installing Xamarin for Mobile App Development

    o   Xamarin is included in Visual Studio if you selected the **Mobile development with .NET** workload. You can start building iOS and Android apps with a shared C# codebase.

    o   If using Visual Studio for Mac, Xamarin is already integrated. You can check that it is installed by opening the Visual Studio for Mac and creating a new Xamarin mobile project.

Using IDEs for Development

Integrated Development Environments (IDEs) are essential tools for developers. They provide features like syntax highlighting, code completion, debugging, and project management, which are invaluable when developing complex applications.

Popular IDEs for Python

1. **PyCharm**
   o **PyCharm** is one of the best IDEs for Python development. It provides support for web development frameworks (like Flask and Django), testing frameworks, and also integrates with version control systems like **Git**. It's available in a **Community Edition** (free) and a **Professional Edition** (paid).
   o PyCharm also integrates well with virtual environments, so you can manage dependencies for different projects easily.

2. **Visual Studio Code (VS Code)**
   o **VS Code** is a lightweight, open-source IDE that supports multiple languages, including Python. With the Python extension, VS Code provides features like IntelliSense, debugging, and code

navigation. It's highly customizable and supports a wide range of plugins.

3. **Spyder**

   o **Spyder** is an IDE designed for data science and scientific computing. It provides features such as an interactive console, variable explorer, and integrated plotting.

Popular IDEs for C#

1. **Visual Studio**

   o **Visual Studio** is the go-to IDE for C# development. It supports a wide range of languages and platforms (including .NET Core, Xamarin for mobile apps, and more). It offers rich debugging and profiling tools, as well as seamless integration with version control.

2. **Visual Studio Code**

   o **VS Code** is also widely used for C# development. While it's a lightweight editor, you can install the **C# extension** to enable support for C# features such as IntelliSense, debugging, and project management. It's suitable for smaller C# projects or cross-platform development with .NET Core.

Setting Up Version Control

Version control is a critical aspect of modern software development, enabling you to track changes, collaborate with others, and maintain a history of your code.

Setting Up Git for Version Control

1. **Installing Git**
   - o **Git** is the most commonly used version control system in the software development industry. You can download and install Git from the official website (Git Downloads).

2. **Setting Up Git for the First Time**
   - o After installing Git, set up your global username and email:

   ```bash
   git config --global user.name "Your Name"
   git config --global user.email "your.email@example.com"
   ```

3. **Creating a Git Repository**
   - o To create a Git repository for your project, navigate to your project folder in the terminal and initialize Git:

```bash
git init
```

4. Connecting to Remote Repositories

o If you want to push your code to a remote repository (e.g., GitHub, GitLab, Bitbucket), create a repository on the respective platform and link it to your local project:

```bash
git remote add origin https://github.com/yourusername/yourrepository.git
```

5. Committing and Pushing Changes

o Stage changes for commit:

```bash
git add .
```

o Commit changes:

```bash
git commit -m "Initial commit"
```

o Push to the remote repository:

```bash
bash
```

```bash
git push -u origin master
```

Essential Tools for Python and C#

- **Docker**: For containerizing your application and ensuring consistency across different environments. This is particularly useful when testing and deploying your cross-platform app.
- **Postman**: For testing APIs and ensuring smooth communication between different parts of your app.
- **TestRunners (pytest for Python, NUnit for C#)**: For automating your tests and ensuring that your code works correctly across platforms.

Conclusion

Setting up a local development environment for Python and C# is the first step towards building cross-platform applications. By installing the right tools—such as Python, C#, Visual Studio, PyCharm, and Git—you can streamline your workflow and improve productivity. Additionally, setting up version control ensures that your code is always tracked, and you can collaborate efficiently with others. With the right development environment in place, you'll be ready to tackle cross-platform app development with confidence.

CHAPTER 5

BUILDING YOUR FIRST CROSS-PLATFORM APPLICATION

In this chapter, we'll walk you through the process of building a basic cross-platform application using both **Python** and **C#**. This will give you a hands-on experience in understanding how to leverage these languages and frameworks to create applications that can run seamlessly on **Windows**, **macOS**, and **Linux**.

We'll use simple tools and frameworks to create a basic "Hello World" application, demonstrating how to set up a basic interface and ensure your application runs across different platforms.

Part 1: Building Your First Cross-Platform Application in Python

We will build a basic **GUI** application using **Kivy**, a Python framework that supports cross-platform development.

Step 1: Setting Up the Environment for Python

1. **Install Python**: Ensure that Python is installed on your system. You can download it from the official Python website (python.org).

2. **Install Kivy**: Open your terminal and install **Kivy** using `pip`:

```bash
pip install kivy
```

3. **Create a New Project**: Create a new directory for your project and navigate to it:

```bash
mkdir hello_world_app
cd hello_world_app
```

Step 2: Writing the Application Code

Create a new Python file named `main.py` in your project directory. This file will contain the basic code for the app.

```python
from kivy.app import App
from kivy.uix.label import Label
```

44

```
class HelloWorldApp(App):
    def build(self):
        return Label(text="Hello, World!")

if __name__ == "__main__":
    HelloWorldApp().run()
```

Explanation:

- `App`: This is the main class in Kivy for creating an application.
- `Label`: A basic widget that displays text on the screen.
- The `build()` method returns a `Label` widget with the text "Hello, World!".

Step 3: Running the Application

To run your application, open the terminal in the project directory and execute:

```
bash
```

```
python main.py
```

The application will open a window displaying the text "Hello, World!" You should see the same behavior whether

45

you're on **Windows**, **macOS**, or **Linux** as Kivy handles the cross-platform aspects automatically.

Part 2: Building Your First Cross-Platform Application in C#

Now, let's build the same "Hello World" application using **C#** and **Xamarin.Forms**, which is ideal for building cross-platform mobile applications.

Step 1: Setting Up the Environment for C#

1. **Install Visual Studio**: Download and install **Visual Studio** from Microsoft's website. During the installation, make sure to select the **Mobile development with .NET** workload to get Xamarin support.
2. **Create a New Xamarin.Forms Project**: After opening Visual Studio, create a new **Xamarin.Forms** project:
   o Select **File > New > Project**.
   o Choose **Mobile App (Xamarin.Forms)**.
   o Select **Blank App** (this will give us a basic template to work with).

Step 2: Writing the Application Code

In the **MainPage.xaml** file, add the following code:

xml

```
<?xml version="1.0" encoding="utf-8" ?>
<ContentPage
xmlns="http://xamarin.com/schemas/2014/forms"

xmlns:x="http://schemas.microsoft.com/winfx/200
6/xaml"
          x:Class="HelloWorldApp.MainPage">

    <StackLayout>
        <!-- A Label to display "Hello, World!"
-->
        <Label Text="Hello, World!"

VerticalOptions="CenterAndExpand"

HorizontalOptions="CenterAndExpand" />
    </StackLayout>

</ContentPage>
```

Explanation:

- This XAML code creates a simple user interface with a Label displaying "Hello, World!" in the center of the screen.

- The StackLayout is a container that stacks its children vertically.

47

Next, in **MainPage.xaml.cs**, the code behind will be automatically generated for you. If needed, you can add event handlers or additional logic here, but for now, we leave it as is since Xamarin takes care of handling platform-specific requirements.

Step 3: Running the Application

To run the application:

1. Select an emulator or connect a mobile device to your computer.
2. In Visual Studio, click on **Start Debugging** (or press F5) to deploy and run the application.

You should now see the "Hello, World!" message on your mobile emulator or device, whether it's running **iOS** or **Android**. Xamarin will handle the cross-platform deployment and rendering, allowing your app to look and behave similarly across both platforms.

Part 3: Testing Your Application on Multiple Platforms

Testing across different platforms ensures that your application runs correctly on all target devices. Here's how you can test your cross-platform apps on **Windows**, **macOS**, and **Linux**.

Testing the Python Application (Kivy) on Multiple Platforms

1. **Windows**:
   - o Simply run the Python app as shown earlier. If you're on Windows, ensure that your dependencies are installed (e.g., Kivy and any platform-specific requirements).

2. **macOS**:
   - o Install Python and Kivy as discussed above.
   - o Once installed, open your terminal, navigate to the project directory, and run the Python script as you did on Windows:

   ```bash
   bash
   ```

   ```
   python main.py
   ```

3. **Linux**:
   - o For Linux, you can follow the same steps. If you're using Ubuntu, you may need to install some additional dependencies for Kivy:

   ```bash
   bash
   ```

   ```
   sudo apt-get install python3-pip
   python3-dev build-essential
   sudo apt-get install libgl1-mesa-glx
   libgles2-mesa
   ```

o Then, run the Python application:

```bash

python main.py
```

Testing the C# Application (Xamarin) on Multiple Platforms

1. **Windows**:

   o Run your Xamarin app in Visual Studio. Use the Android emulator for testing or connect a physical device via USB.

2. **macOS**:

   o You can also run the Xamarin app on macOS using the **iOS Simulator** or a connected iOS device. Visual Studio for Mac provides a similar setup to Visual Studio on Windows, making it easy to deploy apps on both Android and iOS.

3. **Linux**:

   o While Xamarin is primarily geared for mobile development on iOS and Android, testing on Linux isn't officially supported for mobile apps. However, you can use **.NET Core** to build cross-platform desktop apps and test them on Linux by running them directly via the terminal:

   ```bash
   ```

```
dotnet run
```

Conclusion

In this chapter, we've walked through building a basic "Hello World" application using both Python (with Kivy) and C# (with Xamarin). You've learned how to:

- Set up the development environment for both Python and C#.
- Write and run your first cross-platform application.
- Test your application on multiple platforms including Windows, macOS, and Linux.

By mastering these basic steps, you've laid the foundation for developing more complex cross-platform applications using both Python and C#.

CHAPTER 6

INTEGRATING THIRD-PARTY LIBRARIES AND APIS

Integrating third-party libraries and APIs (Application Programming Interfaces) is a critical step in enhancing the functionality and user experience of your cross-platform applications. Libraries and APIs allow you to extend the capabilities of your application without having to build everything from scratch. This chapter will guide you through the process of integrating third-party libraries and APIs in both Python and C#, and provide real-world examples of common integrations, such as **social media** and **payment gateways**.

Part 1: Enhancing Your Applications with Third-Party Libraries

Python: Using Libraries to Extend Application Functionality

Python's vast ecosystem of libraries and packages makes it easy to add additional features to your applications. These libraries are often open-source, meaning you can freely download and use them in your projects.

How to Install Python Libraries: To install a third-party library in Python, you can use **pip**, the Python package installer:

```bash
```

```
pip install library-name
```

For instance, to install a library like **requests** (used for making HTTP requests):

```bash
```

```
pip install requests
```

Common Python Libraries:

- **Requests**: For making HTTP requests to communicate with web services.
- **Flask/Django**: Frameworks for building web applications.
- **Pillow**: For image processing.
- **SQLAlchemy**: For database integration.

Example: Using the **Requests** library to access an API.

```python
```

```
import requests
```

53

```
# Example: Fetch data from a public API
url                                        =
"https://jsonplaceholder.typicode.com/posts"
response = requests.get(url)

if response.status_code == 200:
    data = response.json()
    print(data)
else:
    print("Failed to retrieve data")
```

This simple Python script uses the `requests` library to fetch data from a placeholder API and print it. You can use similar techniques to integrate APIs for social media, payment gateways, or other services.

C#: Using Libraries to Enhance Your Application

In C#, third-party libraries are often distributed through **NuGet**, a package manager for the .NET ecosystem. You can add libraries to your project directly from Visual Studio.

How to Install Libraries via NuGet:

1. In Visual Studio, right-click on your project in the Solution Explorer.
2. Select **Manage NuGet Packages**.

3. Search for the package you want to install and click **Install**.

Alternatively, you can use the NuGet Package Manager Console to install packages:

```bash
Install-Package library-name
```

Common C# Libraries:

- **Newtonsoft.Json**: For working with JSON data.
- **RestSharp**: For making HTTP requests to external APIs.
- **Entity Framework**: For database access.
- **Xamarin.Essentials**: Provides cross-platform APIs for mobile apps.

Example: Using **RestSharp** to make an API request.

```csharp
using RestSharp;
using Newtonsoft.Json;
using System;

public class APIExample
{
    public void FetchData()
```

```csharp
{
    var client = new
RestClient("https://jsonplaceholder.typicode.co
m/posts");
    var request = new
RestRequest(Method.GET);

    IRestResponse response =
client.Execute(request);

    if (response.IsSuccessful)
    {
        var data =
JsonConvert.DeserializeObject(response.Content)
;
        Console.WriteLine(data);
    }
    else
    {
        Console.WriteLine("Failed to
retrieve data");
    }
}
}
```

In this C# example, we use **RestSharp** to send a GET request to an API, and **Newtonsoft.Json** to deserialize the JSON response.

Part 2: Real-World Examples of API Integrations

Now, let's walk through two real-world examples: integrating **social media** APIs and **payment gateway** APIs into your applications.

Example 1: Social Media API Integration

Let's say you want to integrate **Twitter** functionality into your app, allowing users to post tweets directly from your application.

Step 1: Create a Twitter Developer Account

- Go to the Twitter Developer portal.
- Create an app and get your API keys (Consumer Key, Consumer Secret, Access Token, and Access Token Secret).

Step 2: Using Tweepy (Python Library for Twitter API)

To interact with Twitter's API in Python, you can use the **Tweepy** library.

1. **Install Tweepy**:

    bash

```
pip install tweepy
```

2. **Example: Posting a Tweet using Tweepy**:

```python
python

import tweepy

# Authentication credentials
consumer_key = 'your-consumer-key'
consumer_secret = 'your-consumer-secret'
access_token = 'your-access-token'
access_token_secret = 'your-access-token-secret'

# Authenticate to Twitter
auth = tweepy.OAuth1UserHandler(consumer_key,
consumer_secret,                        access_token,
access_token_secret)
api = tweepy.API(auth)

# Post a Tweet
api.update_status("Hello, World! This is a tweet
from my Python app.")
print("Tweet posted successfully!")
```

This Python script allows you to authenticate with Twitter using the credentials you got from the developer portal and post a tweet. You can extend this example to fetch tweets, reply to them, or follow users.

Example 2: Payment Gateway Integration (Stripe)

For many applications, integrating payment gateways is a critical feature. **Stripe** is a popular payment platform that allows you to process payments in your app.

Step 1: Set Up Stripe Account

- Sign up for a **Stripe** account at stripe.com.
- After creating an account, obtain your **API keys** (publishable key and secret key).

Step 2: Using Stripe API in Python

1. **Install Stripe Python Library**:

bash

```
pip install stripe
```

2. **Example: Processing Payments with Stripe in Python**:

python

```
import stripe

# Set your secret key
stripe.api_key = 'your-secret-key'
```

59

```
# Create a payment intent
payment_intent = stripe.PaymentIntent.create(
    amount=1000,  # Amount in cents
    currency='usd',
)
```

```
print(f"Payment        Intent        Created:
{payment_intent.id}")
```

This script initializes the **Stripe API** and creates a **PaymentIntent**, which is used to handle a payment. In a real application, you would typically integrate this with a front-end payment form (using Stripe's **Checkout** or **Elements**) to collect payment information from the user.

Step 3: Using Stripe API in C#

1. **Install Stripe.Net** (Stripe's C# SDK) via NuGet:

   ```bash
   Install-Package Stripe.net
   ```

2. **Example: Processing Payments in C#**:

```csharp
using Stripe;
```

```csharp
using System;

public class StripeExample
{
    public void ProcessPayment()
    {
        StripeConfiguration.ApiKey   =   "your-
secret-key";

        var        options      =        new
PaymentIntentCreateOptions
        {
            Amount = 1000,   // Amount in cents
            Currency = "usd",
        };

        var        service      =        new
PaymentIntentService();
        PaymentIntent        intent        =
service.Create(options);

        Console.WriteLine($"Payment        Intent
Created: {intent.Id}");
    }
}
```

In this C# example, we use the **Stripe.net** library to create a payment intent and send the information to the Stripe API.

Conclusion

Integrating third-party libraries and APIs is a powerful way to enhance the functionality of your cross-platform applications. Whether you're adding **social media** features or integrating a **payment gateway** like **Stripe**, these integrations allow you to provide rich, modern functionality to your users. In Python, libraries like **Tweepy** and **Requests** make integration straightforward, while in C#, libraries like **RestSharp** and **Stripe.net** help you interact with external services efficiently.

By mastering these integrations, you can extend the capabilities of your applications, streamline development, and offer valuable features that improve the user experience.

CHAPTER 7

DATA HANDLING AND STORAGE SOLUTIONS

Effective data handling and storage are essential components of any cross-platform application. Managing data, especially across multiple platforms, requires a consistent approach to ensure that users have access to their data at all times, regardless of the device or operating system they're using. In this chapter, we'll explore how to work with databases in cross-platform apps, synchronize data between platforms, and look at real-world examples using popular databases like **SQLite** and **PostgreSQL**.

Part 1: Working with Databases in Cross-Platform Apps

1. SQLite in Cross-Platform Applications

SQLite is a popular, lightweight, serverless, self-contained SQL database engine that is commonly used in mobile and desktop applications. It's an excellent choice for cross-platform applications because it's easy to set up and doesn't require a separate server to manage the data.

63

Setting Up SQLite in Python

SQLite comes bundled with Python's standard library, so you don't need to install anything extra. Here's how you can use SQLite in Python:

1. **Creating a Database**:

```python
import sqlite3

# Connect to SQLite database (it will be
created if it doesn't exist)
conn = sqlite3.connect('example.db')

# Create a cursor object to interact with
the database
cursor = conn.cursor()

# Create a table
cursor.execute('''CREATE   TABLE   IF   NOT
EXISTS users
                (id INTEGER PRIMARY KEY,
name TEXT, age INTEGER)''')

# Insert some data
cursor.execute("INSERT   INTO   users   (name,
age) VALUES ('Alice', 30)")
```

```
cursor.execute("INSERT  INTO  users  (name,
age) VALUES ('Bob', 25)")

# Commit changes and close the connection
conn.commit()
conn.close()
```

2. **Reading Data**:

```python
python
```

```python
conn = sqlite3.connect('example.db')
cursor = conn.cursor()

cursor.execute("SELECT * FROM users")
rows = cursor.fetchall()
for row in rows:
    print(row)

conn.close()
```

This code snippet creates an SQLite database, inserts data, and retrieves it. Because SQLite is file-based, the same database file (example.db) can be shared and accessed across different platforms.

Setting Up SQLite in C#

In C#, SQLite can be used via the **System.Data.SQLite** library, which you can install through NuGet.

1. **Install SQLite NuGet Package**:

```bash
bash

Install-Package System.Data.SQLite
```

2. **Creating a Database**:

```csharp
csharp

using System;
using System.Data.SQLite;

class Program
{
    static void Main()
    {
        // Create a new database or connect to an existing one
        using (var connection = new SQLiteConnection("Data Source=example.db;Version=3;"))
        {
            connection.Open();
```

```csharp
// Create a table
string createTable = "CREATE
TABLE IF NOT EXISTS users (id INTEGER
PRIMARY KEY, name TEXT, age INTEGER)";
using (var command = new
SQLiteCommand(createTable, connection))
{

command.ExecuteNonQuery();
}

// Insert data
string insertData = "INSERT
INTO users (name, age) VALUES ('Alice',
30)";
using (var command = new
SQLiteCommand(insertData, connection))
{

command.ExecuteNonQuery();
}

connection.Close();
}
}
}
```

3. **Reading Data**:

```csharp
using (var connection = new
SQLiteConnection("Data
Source=example.db;Version=3;"))
{
    connection.Open();
    string query = "SELECT * FROM users";
    using (var command = new
SQLiteCommand(query, connection))
    {
        using (SQLiteDataReader reader =
command.ExecuteReader())
        {
            while (reader.Read())
            {
                Console.WriteLine($"ID:
{reader["id"]}, Name: {reader["name"]},
Age: {reader["age"]}");
            }
        }
    }
}
```

This C# code works similarly to the Python example, creating an SQLite database, inserting records, and retrieving data. SQLite is platform-independent, so you can easily use the same code on different operating systems.

2. PostgreSQL in Cross-Platform Applications

PostgreSQL is a powerful, open-source relational database system. It is more suitable for applications requiring complex queries and high performance than SQLite. It can be used in a cross-platform application by setting up a PostgreSQL server or using a cloud-based PostgreSQL solution (such as **Heroku Postgres** or **AWS RDS**).

Setting Up PostgreSQL in Python

To work with PostgreSQL in Python, you can use the **psycopg2** library.

1. **Install psycopg2**:

```bash
bash
```

```bash
pip install psycopg2
```

2. **Connecting to PostgreSQL**:

```python
python
```

```python
import psycopg2

# Establish a connection to the PostgreSQL
server
```

```python
conn = psycopg2.connect(dbname="testdb",
user="yourusername",
password="yourpassword", host="localhost",
port="5432")

# Create a cursor object to interact with
the database
cursor = conn.cursor()

# Create a table
cursor.execute('''CREATE TABLE IF NOT
EXISTS users (id SERIAL PRIMARY KEY, name
VARCHAR(100), age INT)''')

# Insert data
cursor.execute("INSERT INTO users (name,
age) VALUES ('Alice', 30), ('Bob', 25)")

# Commit changes and close the connection
conn.commit()
conn.close()
```

3. Reading Data:

```python
python

conn = psycopg2.connect(dbname="testdb",
user="yourusername",
password="yourpassword", host="localhost",
port="5432")
```

```
cursor = conn.cursor()

cursor.execute("SELECT * FROM users")
rows = cursor.fetchall()
for row in rows:
    print(row)

conn.close()
```

Setting Up PostgreSQL in C#

To interact with PostgreSQL in C#, you can use the **Npgsql** library.

1. **Install Npgsql** via NuGet:

```bash
bash
```

```
Install-Package Npgsql
```

2. **Connecting to PostgreSQL**:

```csharp
csharp
```

```
using Npgsql;
using System;

class Program
{
    static void Main()
```

71

```
{
    string         connString         =
"Host=localhost;Username=yourusername;Pas
sword=yourpassword;Database=testdb";
    using     (var     conn     =     new
NpgsqlConnection(connString))
    {
        conn.Open();

        // Create a table
        using    (var    cmd    =    new
NpgsqlCommand("CREATE TABLE IF NOT EXISTS
users   (id   SERIAL   PRIMARY   KEY,   name
VARCHAR(100), age INT)", conn))
        {
            cmd.ExecuteNonQuery();
        }

        // Insert data
        using    (var    cmd    =    new
NpgsqlCommand("INSERT   INTO   users   (name,
age) VALUES ('Alice', 30), ('Bob', 25)",
conn))
        {
            cmd.ExecuteNonQuery();
        }

        conn.Close();
    }
```

```
    }
}
```

3. **Reading Data**:

csharp

```
string            connString        =
"Host=localhost;Username=yourusername;Pas
sword=yourpassword;Database=testdb";
using     (var     conn    =      new
NpgsqlConnection(connString))
{
    conn.Open();
    using     (var    cmd    =     new
NpgsqlCommand("SELECT   *   FROM   users",
conn))
    using      (var      reader     =
cmd.ExecuteReader())
    {
        while (reader.Read())
        {
            Console.WriteLine($"ID:
{reader["id"]},   Name:   {reader["name"]},
Age: {reader["age"]}");
        }
    }
}
```

73

Part 2: Data Synchronization Between Platforms

Data synchronization ensures that information is consistent across multiple platforms or devices. This is especially important in cross-platform applications where users may access the same data on different devices.

1. Local Storage Sync with Cloud (SQLite to PostgreSQL)

One approach to synchronization is to store data locally on the device using **SQLite** and synchronize it with a cloud database (like **PostgreSQL**) when the device is online. This is useful for mobile applications where users can interact with the app offline and sync data when they regain internet access.

2. Using REST APIs for Synchronization

You can use a REST API to sync data between local storage and a remote database.

Python Example (Syncing SQLite data to PostgreSQL using a REST API):

```python
python

import requests
```

```python
import sqlite3

# Fetch data from SQLite
conn = sqlite3.connect('example.db')
cursor = conn.cursor()
cursor.execute("SELECT * FROM users")
rows = cursor.fetchall()

# Send data to a remote PostgreSQL database via
REST API
url = "https://yourapi.com/sync"
for row in rows:
    payload = {'name': row[1], 'age': row[2]}
    response = requests.post(url, json=payload)
    print(response.status_code)

conn.close()
```

This example fetches data from an SQLite database and sends it to a remote PostgreSQL server using a REST API.

Part 3: Real-World Examples with SQLite and PostgreSQL

SQLite in a Mobile App: A mobile app might store user preferences or cached data locally in an SQLite database, allowing for offline functionality. When the user is online, the app could sync this data to a cloud-based PostgreSQL database.

PostgreSQL in a Web App: A web application might use PostgreSQL to manage user accounts and transactions. Data from the web app can be synced with a local SQLite database when the user is offline, and updated data can be pushed to PostgreSQL once the user is back online.

Conclusion

In this chapter, we've explored how to work with databases in cross-platform applications, focusing on **SQLite** for local storage and **PostgreSQL** for cloud-based or centralized databases. We also discussed **data synchronization** strategies, including the use of REST APIs to sync data between local storage and cloud services. These techniques allow you to build robust, scalable applications that work seamlessly across different platforms and ensure that users always have access to their data, whether they're online or offline.

CHAPTER 8

USER INTERFACE DESIGN ACROSS PLATFORMS

Designing a user interface (UI) for multiple platforms can be a challenging task, as each platform—whether it's **Windows**, **macOS**, **iOS**, or **Android**—has its unique design guidelines and user expectations. However, by using cross-platform UI tools like **Xamarin.Forms** for C# and **PyQt** for Python, you can create a unified and seamless experience across devices while adhering to each platform's design principles. In this chapter, we'll explore best practices for designing cross-platform UIs, dive into tools like **Xamarin.Forms** and **PyQt**, and look at a real-world example of a simple yet effective UI design.

Part 1: Best Practices for Designing UI for Multiple Platforms

When designing UIs for multiple platforms, it's crucial to balance **consistency** and **adaptability**. Your app should feel familiar to users regardless of the platform, but it should also adapt to the nuances of each operating system and device.

1. Consistency Across Platforms

- **Design Language**: While each platform has its design language (e.g., **Material Design** for Android, **Human Interface Guidelines** for iOS, and **Windows Fluent Design** for Windows), maintaining a consistent layout and structure is important. For example, keeping the placement of key elements such as navigation buttons, content, and interactive elements consistent across platforms ensures that users can intuitively navigate the app.

- **Branding**: Your branding (colors, fonts, and logos) should be consistent across all platforms. Make sure to design with a consistent color palette and typography that works well on all platforms.

- **Simple Navigation**: Consistency in navigation (e.g., using a hamburger menu on mobile apps or a navigation bar for desktop apps) enhances usability. Ensure that navigational patterns are familiar to the platform's user base.

2. Adapting to Platform-Specific Guidelines

- **iOS**: iOS apps tend to have a minimalistic design, with emphasis on clarity and simplicity. When designing UIs for iOS, use the **Human Interface Guidelines** (HIG) to ensure that the UI aligns with the platform's expectations.

- **Android**: Android apps use **Material Design**, which emphasizes the use of grids, shadows, and animations to create a more tactile feel. Ensure that elements like buttons, text fields, and sliders follow Material Design principles.

- **Desktop (Windows/macOS/Linux)**: Desktop UIs often benefit from more real estate, so you can present more content and make use of features like side navigation bars or tabs. Keep in mind each platform's expectations for windowing, resizing, and navigation.

3. Responsive Layouts

- Cross-platform UIs need to be responsive, meaning they should automatically adjust based on screen size, resolution, and device orientation. Responsive design is especially important for mobile apps, where screen sizes vary widely between phones and tablets.

- Use flexible layouts (e.g., grids, stacks, and percentage-based widths) to make sure your app looks good on all screen sizes.

4. Touch vs. Mouse Interactions

- On mobile devices, touch interactions are the norm, so buttons and interactive elements should be larger and spaced out to make touch interactions easier.

- On desktop platforms, the mouse or trackpad is the primary input device, so UI elements can be smaller and more densely packed.
- Always consider the platform's input methods to make your UI feel natural and intuitive.

Part 2: Tools for Cross-Platform UI Design

1. Xamarin.Forms (C#)

Xamarin.Forms is a cross-platform UI toolkit for C# developers, designed for building mobile apps with a single codebase for both **Android** and **iOS**. Xamarin provides a range of UI controls that adapt automatically to each platform's design guidelines, making it easier to design native-looking apps.

- **Advantages**:
  - **Single Codebase**: Write UI code once and deploy it across both Android and iOS.
  - **Native Performance**: Xamarin compiles to native code, ensuring optimal performance.
  - **Access to Native APIs**: Xamarin allows you to access platform-specific APIs when needed.
- **Example of Xamarin.Forms Code**:

```
csharp
```

```csharp
using Xamarin.Forms;

public class MainPage : ContentPage
{
    public MainPage()
    {
        var button = new Button
        {
            Text = "Click Me",
            VerticalOptions            =
LayoutOptions.Center,
            HorizontalOptions          =
LayoutOptions.Center
        };

        button.Clicked += (sender, e) =>
        {
            DisplayAlert("Alert",  "Button
clicked!", "OK");
        };

        Content = new StackLayout
        {
            Children = { button }
        };
    }
}
```

This simple Xamarin app creates a button that, when clicked, displays an alert. Xamarin automatically adapts this button to look and behave appropriately on both Android and iOS devices.

2. PyQt (Python)

PyQt is a set of Python bindings for the **Qt** application framework, which allows you to build cross-platform desktop apps. PyQt provides a range of powerful widgets and tools for designing native UIs that work on **Windows**, **macOS**, and **Linux**.

- **Advantages**:
    - o **Cross-Platform**: Build applications that run on all major desktop platforms.
    - o **Rich Set of Widgets**: PyQt provides many widgets, including buttons, text boxes, tables, and more.
    - o **Customizable**: You can create highly customizable UIs using PyQt's flexibility.
- **Example of PyQt Code**:

```python

import sys
```

```python
from PyQt5.QtWidgets import QApplication,
QWidget, QPushButton

class App(QWidget):
    def __init__(self):
        super().__init__()
        self.setWindowTitle('Simple    PyQt
App')
        self.setGeometry(100,   100,   300,
200)

        # Create a button and connect it to
a function
        button = QPushButton('Click   Me',
self)

button.clicked.connect(self.on_click)
        button.resize(button.sizeHint())
        button.move(100, 70)

    def on_click(self):
        print("Button clicked!")

if __name__ == '__main__':
    app = QApplication(sys.argv)
    window = App()
    window.show()
    sys.exit(app.exec_())
```

This example creates a simple window with a clickable button. PyQt automatically adapts the UI for each platform while allowing developers to customize the design.

Part 3: Example of a Simple but Effective UI Design

Let's combine the concepts we've discussed into a simple, yet effective, cross-platform UI design for both mobile and desktop applications. The UI will consist of a **header**, a **main content area**, and a **footer** with navigation options.

Design Concept:

- **Header**: Displays the app title.
- **Main Content**: Contains a simple form with a label and a button.
- **Footer**: Displays navigation options (home, settings).

Xamarin.Forms Example:

csharp

```csharp
using Xamarin.Forms;

public class MainPage : ContentPage
{
    public MainPage()
    {
        var header = new Label
```

```csharp
    {
        Text = "My App",
        FontSize = 24,
        HorizontalOptions                    =
LayoutOptions.Center,
        Padding = new Thickness(10)
    };

    var button = new Button
    {
        Text = "Submit",
        VerticalOptions                      =
LayoutOptions.Center,
        HorizontalOptions                    =
LayoutOptions.Center
    };

    var footer = new StackLayout
    {
        Orientation                          =
StackOrientation.Horizontal,
        Children =
        {
            new Button { Text = "Home" },
            new Button { Text = "Settings" }
        },
        Spacing = 20
    };
```

```
        Content = new StackLayout
        {
            Children = { header, button, footer
},
            Padding = new Thickness(20)
        };
    }
}
```

PyQt Example:

python

```python
import sys
from PyQt5.QtWidgets import QApplication,
QWidget, QVBoxLayout, QPushButton, QLabel,
QHBoxLayout

class App(QWidget):
    def __init__(self):
        super().__init__()
        self.setWindowTitle('My App')
        self.setGeometry(100, 100, 300, 200)

        # Header
        header = QLabel('My App', self)
        header.setAlignment(Qt.AlignCenter)
        header.setStyleSheet("font-size:   24px;
padding: 10px;")

        # Button
```

```
        button = QPushButton('Submit', self)

        # Footer with Navigation
        footer = QHBoxLayout()
        footer.addWidget(QPushButton('Home',
self))

footer.addWidget(QPushButton('Settings', self))

        # Layout
        layout = QVBoxLayout()
        layout.addWidget(header)
        layout.addWidget(button)
        layout.addLayout(footer)
        self.setLayout(layout)

if __name__ == '__main__':
    app = QApplication(sys.argv)
    window = App()
    window.show()
    sys.exit(app.exec_())
```

In both examples, the UI has the same structure:

- A header at the top displaying the app's title.
- A button for interaction.
- A footer with navigation options.

This design is simple but effective, ensuring that the user can easily navigate the app regardless of the platform.

Conclusion

Designing user interfaces across multiple platforms requires careful attention to consistency, responsiveness, and platform-specific guidelines. Tools like **Xamarin.Forms** for C# and **PyQt** for Python enable you to create cross-platform UIs that feel native on Android, iOS, Windows, macOS, and Linux. By following best practices and using these tools, you can create intuitive, responsive, and visually appealing UIs that enhance the user experience across all devices.

CHAPTER 9

ADVANCED FEATURES: HANDLING FILE SYSTEMS AND NETWORK REQUESTS

In this chapter, we'll dive into advanced topics related to file handling, directories, and network requests in cross-platform development. Whether you're working with files on the user's device or making API requests to external servers, understanding how to handle these tasks in a way that works seamlessly across platforms is crucial. We will explore how to manage files and directories in both Python and C#, and how to make API requests and handle responses efficiently.

Part 1: Working with Files and Directories Across Different Platforms

File system handling can vary between operating systems due to different directory structures, permissions, and file path conventions. Therefore, writing cross-platform code that can interact with files and directories seamlessly is essential.

1. Working with Files and Directories in Python

Python provides robust tools for handling files and directories, and it automatically handles many platform-specific differences.

1.1 File Operations in Python

Python's **os** and **shutil** modules allow you to work with files and directories across platforms, abstracting the differences between operating systems.

1. **Reading and Writing Files**:

   python

   ```python
   # Writing to a file
   with open('example.txt', 'w') as file:
       file.write('Hello, World!')

   # Reading from a file
   with open('example.txt', 'r') as file:
       content = file.read()
       print(content)
   ```

2. **Checking File Existence**:

   python

```
import os

# Check if a file exists
if os.path.exists('example.txt'):
    print("File exists.")
else:
    print("File does not exist.")
```

3. **Working with Directories**:

```python
```

```
import os

# Create a directory
os.makedirs('my_folder', exist_ok=True)

# List files in a directory
files = os.listdir('.')
print(files)
```

4. **Cross-Platform Paths**: Use `os.path.join()` to create file paths that work across different platforms:

```python
```

```
import os

path      =      os.path.join('my_folder',
'example.txt')
```

```python
print(path)
```

1.2 Directory Management:

- Use **shutil** to , move, or delete files and directories:

```python
python

import shutil

#  file
shutil.('example.txt',
'my_folder/example.txt')

# Delete file
os.remove('example.txt')
```

2. Working with Files and Directories in C#

In C#, file and directory management is handled through the **System.IO** namespace, which provides classes for working with files and directories in a cross-platform manner.

1. **Reading and Writing Files**:

```csharp
csharp

using System;
using System.IO;
```

```
class Program
{
    static void Main()
    {
        // Writing to a file
        File.WriteAllText("example.txt",
"Hello, World!");

        // Reading from a file
        string        content        =
File.ReadAllText("example.txt");
        Console.WriteLine(content);
    }
}
```

2. Checking File Existence:

csharp

```
if (File.Exists("example.txt"))
{
    Console.WriteLine("File exists.");
}
else
{
    Console.WriteLine("File    does    not
exist.");
}
```

3. Creating Directories:

93

```csharp
Directory.CreateDirectory("my_folder");

// List files in a directory
string[] files = Directory.GetFiles(".");
foreach (string file in files)
{
    Console.WriteLine(file);
}
```

4. **Cross-Platform Paths**: C# provides `Path.Combine()` to create platform-independent file paths:

```csharp
string path = Path.Combine("my_folder",
"example.txt");
Console.WriteLine(path);
```

5. **ing and Deleting Files**:

```csharp
// file
File.("example.txt",
"my_folder/example.txt");
```

```
// Delete file
File.Delete("example.txt");
```

Part 2: Making API Requests and Handling Responses in Python and C#

API requests allow your applications to fetch data from external servers or services. Whether you're retrieving information from a remote server or submitting data, understanding how to make requests and handle responses is key for modern cross-platform apps.

1. Making API Requests in Python

Python provides the **requests** library, which makes it easy to send HTTP requests to a server and handle the responses.

1.1 Installing Requests Library:

```bash
pip install requests
```

1.2 Making GET and POST Requests:

```python
import requests
```

```python
# GET request
response = requests.get('https://jsonplaceholder.typicode.com/posts/1')
if response.status_code == 200:
    data = response.json()
    print(data)


# POST request
payload = {'title': 'foo', 'body': 'bar', 'userId': 1}
response = requests.post('https://jsonplaceholder.typicode.com/posts', json=payload)
if response.status_code == 201:
    print(response.json())
```

- **GET request**: Used for fetching data from the server.
- **POST request**: Used for sending data to the server.

1.3 Handling Response Data:

python

```python
# Extract JSON data from the response
json_data = response.json()
print(json_data)

# Extract specific data
post_title = json_data['title']
```

```
print(post_title)
```

1.4 Handling Errors:

```python
python

try:
    response = requests.get('https://invalid-
url.com')
    response.raise_for_status()  # Raise an error
for bad responses (4xx, 5xx)
except requests.exceptions.RequestException as
e:
    print(f"Error occurred: {e}")
```

2. Making API Requests in C#

In C#, **HttpClient** is the primary class for sending HTTP requests. It's part of the **System.Net.Http** namespace and provides an easy-to-use API for making requests.

2.1 Making GET and POST Requests:

```csharp
csharp

using System;
using System.Net.Http;
using System.Threading.Tasks;

class Program
```

```csharp
{
    static async Task Main()
    {
        // Create an instance of HttpClient
        using (var client = new HttpClient())
        {
            // GET request
            HttpResponseMessage response = await
client.GetAsync("https://jsonplaceholder.typico
de.com/posts/1");
            if (response.IsSuccessStatusCode)
            {
                string    content    =    await
response.Content.ReadAsStringAsync();
                Console.WriteLine(content);
            }

            // POST request
            var        content        =        new
StringContent("{\"title\":\"foo\",\"body\":\"ba
r\",\"userId\":1}",    System.Text.Encoding.UTF8,
"application/json");
            response              =              await
client.PostAsync("https://jsonplaceholder.typic
ode.com/posts", content);
            if (response.IsSuccessStatusCode)
            {
                string    result    =    await
response.Content.ReadAsStringAsync();
```

```
            Console.WriteLine(result);
        }
      }
   }
}
```

2.2 Handling Response Data:

csharp

```
// Parse JSON response
string          jsonData         =          await
response.Content.ReadAsStringAsync();
// Deserialize JSON to a C# object (if necessary)
var            post                =
JsonSerializer.Deserialize<Post>(jsonData);
Console.WriteLine(post.Title);
```

2.3 Handling Errors:

csharp

```
try
{
    HttpResponseMessage   response   =   await
client.GetAsync("https://invalid-url.com");
    response.EnsureSuccessStatusCode();
}
catch (HttpRequestException e)
{
```

```
    Console.WriteLine($"Request          error:
{e.Message}");
}
```

Part 3: Example: Downloading and Saving Data from a Server

Now let's take the concepts we've learned and create an example where we download data from a server and save it to a file.

1. Python Example: Download and Save Data

python

```python
import requests

# Make a GET request to fetch data
url                              =
'https://jsonplaceholder.typicode.com/posts/1'
response = requests.get(url)

# Check if request was successful
if response.status_code == 200:
    # Save the response content to a file
    with open('post_data.json', 'w') as file:
        file.write(response.text)
    print("Data saved to post_data.json")
else:
    print("Failed to retrieve data.")
```

2. C# Example: Download and Save Data

csharp

```csharp
using System;
using System.Net.Http;
using System.IO;
using System.Threading.Tasks;

class Program
{
    static async Task Main()
    {
        string                 url                =
"https://jsonplaceholder.typicode.com/posts/1";

        using (var client = new HttpClient())
        {
            // Make GET request to fetch data
            HttpResponseMessage response = await
client.GetAsync(url);

            if (response.IsSuccessStatusCode)
            {
                // Read the response content
                string    content    =    await
response.Content.ReadAsStringAsync();

                // Save the content to a file
```

```
            await
File.WriteAllTextAsync("post_data.json",
content);
                Console.WriteLine("Data saved to
post_data.json");
            }
            else
            {
                Console.WriteLine("Failed       to
retrieve data.");
            }
        }
    }
}
```

Conclusion

In this chapter, we covered the essential techniques for handling file systems and making network requests in cross-platform applications. By using Python's **os**, **requests** modules, and C#'s **System.IO**, **HttpClient**, you can work with files and make API requests in a way that works seamlessly across platforms. The examples of downloading and saving data from a server showed how to integrate these techniques into real-world scenarios.

CHAPTER 10

SECURITY BEST PRACTICES FOR CROSS-PLATFORM APPS

In cross-platform application development, security is paramount. Your app might be handling sensitive user data, interacting with APIs, or using third-party services, making it vulnerable to various types of attacks if not properly secured. This chapter will explore the key security risks that cross-platform apps face, how to mitigate them, and the best practices for implementing encryption, authentication, and secure data storage across platforms. We'll also look at real-world examples of how security can be implemented in Python and C# apps.

Part 1: Understanding Security Risks and How to Mitigate Them

1. Common Security Risks for Cross-Platform Apps

Cross-platform applications, due to their nature of running on multiple platforms (mobile, desktop, web), are exposed to several unique security risks. Some of the most common security vulnerabilities include:

- **Data Exposure**: If sensitive data is not properly encrypted, it may be exposed to attackers, especially when transmitted over the network or stored locally.

- **Man-in-the-Middle Attacks**: If communications between your app and a server are not encrypted, attackers could intercept and alter the data being transmitted.

- **Insecure Data Storage**: Storing sensitive data, such as passwords or user credentials, on the device without encryption leaves it vulnerable to local attacks.

- **Authentication Weaknesses**: Improper authentication methods or weak passwords can allow unauthorized users to gain access to sensitive resources.

2. Mitigating Security Risks

To mitigate these security risks, you should follow best practices for encryption, secure communication, authentication, and data storage.

- **Use HTTPS for Communication**: Always use **SSL/TLS** (HTTPS) to encrypt communication between the app and the server. This ensures that data is transmitted securely and prevents man-in-the-middle attacks.

- **Encrypt Sensitive Data**: Sensitive data (such as passwords, tokens, and personal information) should never be stored in plaintext. Use encryption algorithms to protect this data both in transit and at rest.

- **Secure Authentication**: Implement strong user authentication using OAuth, JWT (JSON Web Tokens), or multi-factor authentication (MFA) to prevent unauthorized access.

- **Regular Updates and Patches**: Keep your libraries, frameworks, and platforms updated to ensure that known security vulnerabilities are patched.

Part 2: Encryption, Authentication, and Secure Data Storage Across Platforms

1. Encryption Across Platforms

Encryption is essential for protecting sensitive information, both when it is stored locally and during transmission. Below, we cover how to implement encryption in Python and C#.

1.1 Encryption in Python

Python provides several libraries to implement encryption, such as **PyCryptodome** and **cryptography**. We'll use **cryptography** for this example.

Installing cryptography library:

```bash
pip install cryptography
```

Example: Encrypting and Decrypting Data in Python:

```python
from cryptography.fernet import Fernet

# Generate a key for encryption
key = Fernet.generate_key()
cipher = Fernet(key)

# Encrypt data
data = "Sensitive data that needs to be encrypted"
encrypted_data = cipher.encrypt(data.encode())

# Decrypt data
decrypted_data = cipher.decrypt(encrypted_data).decode()
```

```
print(f"Original Data: {data}")
print(f"Encrypted Data: {encrypted_data}")
print(f"Decrypted Data: {decrypted_data}")
```

In this example, we use **Fernet** encryption from the **cryptography** library to encrypt and decrypt data using a symmetric key.

1.2 Encryption in C#

In C#, you can use the **System.Security.Cryptography** namespace for encryption tasks. Below is an example of encrypting and decrypting data using **AES** (Advanced Encryption Standard).

Example: Encrypting and Decrypting Data in C#:

```csharp
csharp

using System;
using System.Security.Cryptography;
using System.Text;

class Program
{
    static void Main()
    {
        // Generate a new AES key
```

```
using (Aes aesAlg = Aes.Create())
{
    aesAlg.GenerateKey();
    aesAlg.GenerateIV();

    // Encrypt data
    string data = "Sensitive data that needs to be encrypted";
    byte[] encryptedData = EncryptData(data, aesAlg.Key, aesAlg.IV);

    // Decrypt data
    string decryptedData = DecryptData(encryptedData, aesAlg.Key, aesAlg.IV);

    Console.WriteLine($"Original Data: {data}");
    Console.WriteLine($"Encrypted Data: {Convert.ToBase64String(encryptedData)}");
    Console.WriteLine($"Decrypted Data: {decryptedData}");
    }
}

static byte[] EncryptData(string data, byte[] key, byte[] iv)
{
    using (Aes aesAlg = Aes.Create())
```

```csharp
{
    aesAlg.Key = key;
    aesAlg.IV = iv;

    ICryptoTransform encryptor = aesAlg.CreateEncryptor(aesAlg.Key, aesAlg.IV);

    using (System.IO.MemoryStream ms = new System.IO.MemoryStream())
    using (CryptoStream cs = new CryptoStream(ms, encryptor, CryptoStreamMode.Write))
    using (System.IO.StreamWriter writer = new System.IO.StreamWriter(cs))
    {
        writer.Write(data);
        return ms.ToArray();
    }
}
}

static string DecryptData(byte[] encryptedData, byte[] key, byte[] iv)
{
    using (Aes aesAlg = Aes.Create())
    {
        aesAlg.Key = key;
        aesAlg.IV = iv;
```

```
        ICryptoTransform      decryptor      =
aesAlg.CreateDecryptor(aesAlg.Key, aesAlg.IV);

        using (System.IO.MemoryStream ms =
new System.IO.MemoryStream(encryptedData))
        using (CryptoStream cs = new
CryptoStream(ms,                decryptor,
CryptoStreamMode.Read))
        using (System.IO.StreamReader reader
= new System.IO.StreamReader(cs))
        {
            return reader.ReadToEnd();
        }
    }
  }
}
```

In this C# example, we use **AES** encryption to encrypt and decrypt data securely.

2. Authentication Across Platforms

Authentication is one of the most critical aspects of app security. Implementing proper authentication ensures that only authorized users can access certain features of the app.

2.1 OAuth Authentication in Python

OAuth 2.0 is a widely-used standard for authorization. Python provides **requests-oauthlib** to implement OAuth authentication in web apps.

Installing requests-oauthlib:

```bash
pip install requests-oauthlib
```

Example: OAuth Authentication in Python:

```python
from requests_oauthlib import OAuth2Session

client_id = 'your-client-id'
client_secret = 'your-client-secret'
authorization_base_url                          =
'https://example.com/oauth/authorize'
token_url = 'https://example.com/oauth/token'

# Create an OAuth2 session
oauth = OAuth2Session(client_id)

# Get authorization URL
authorization_url,              state            =
oauth.authorization_url(authorization_base_url)
```

```
print(f'Please   go   to   {authorization_url}   and
authorize access.')

# After authorization, get the token
redirect_response   =   input('Paste   the   full
redirect URL here: ')
oauth.fetch_token(token_url,
authorization_response=redirect_response,
client_secret=client_secret)

# Make a request to the protected resource
response                                          =
oauth.get('https://example.com/api/user')
print(response.json())
```

This example uses OAuth2 for authentication, allowing users to log in securely to your app via third-party services.

2.2 OAuth Authentication in C#

In C#, you can use **Microsoft.Identity.Client** for OAuth authentication.

Installing Microsoft.Identity.Client via NuGet:

bash

```
Install-Package Microsoft.Identity.Client
```

Example: OAuth Authentication in C#:

csharp

```csharp
using Microsoft.Identity.Client;
using System;
using System.Threading.Tasks;

class Program
{
    static async Task Main(string[] args)
    {
        var cca =
ConfidentialClientApplicationBuilder.Create("yo
ur-client-id")
            .WithClientSecret("your-client-
secret")
            .WithAuthority(new
Uri("https://login.microsoftonline.com/your-
tenant-id"))
            .Build();

        var result = await
cca.AcquireTokenForClient(new[] {
"https://graph.microsoft.com/.default" })
            .ExecuteAsync();

        Console.WriteLine($"Access Token:
{result.AccessToken}");
```

```
    }
}
```

In this C# example, we authenticate a user using OAuth2, acquire an access token, and then use it to make authenticated requests.

3. Secure Data Storage Across Platforms

It's important to store sensitive data, such as passwords, tokens, and encryption keys, securely. Both Python and C# offer solutions for securely storing data across platforms.

3.1 Secure Storage in Python:

In Python, you can use the **keyring** library for securely storing credentials and sensitive data in the system's keychain.

Installing keyring:

```bash
pip install keyring
```

Example: Storing and Retrieving Secrets Using keyring:

```python
```

```
import keyring

# Store a secret
keyring.set_password("my_service",    "username",
"my_secret_password")

# Retrieve the secret
password    =    keyring.get_password("my_service",
"username")
print(password)
```

This ensures that sensitive data like passwords are stored securely in the system's keychain and not in plaintext files.

3.2 Secure Storage in C#:

In C#, you can use **Windows.Security.Credentials** or the **Keychain** API (for macOS) to securely store sensitive data.

Example: Storing and Retrieving Data with Windows Credential Locker:

```csharp

using System;
using Windows.Security.Credentials;

class Program
```

```
{
    static void Main()
    {
        var vault = new PasswordVault();
        vault.Add(new
PasswordCredential("my_service",    "username",
"my_secret_password"));

        // Retrieve the secret
        var             credential              =
vault.Retrieve("my_service", "username");
        Console.WriteLine(credential.Password);
    }
}
```

This example stores credentials securely using the Windows Credential Locker.

Conclusion

Security is crucial when building cross-platform applications, especially when handling sensitive data, user credentials, and authentication. In this chapter, we covered how to mitigate security risks, implement encryption, handle authentication, and store data securely across platforms using Python and C#. By following these best practices, you can ensure that your app remains secure, protecting both user data and your application from potential threats.

CHAPTER 11

CONTINUOUS INTEGRATION AND CONTINUOUS DELIVERY (CI/CD) IN DEVOPS

In modern software development, ensuring that your code is always in a deployable state is crucial for rapid iteration and delivering value to users. This is where **Continuous Integration (CI)** and **Continuous Delivery (CD)** play a key role. CI/CD is a set of practices that automates the processes of testing, building, and deploying applications, ensuring that software is always in a state that can be released to production at any time. This chapter will introduce CI/CD concepts, explain how to implement CI/CD pipelines using **Python**, **C#**, and modern DevOps tools, and walk through a real-world CI/CD pipeline example.

Part 1: Introduction to CI/CD Concepts and Their Importance

1. Continuous Integration (CI)

Continuous Integration is the practice of merging all developers' working copies of code into a shared main branch frequently, ideally multiple times a day. This is done

117

to catch integration issues early, improve collaboration, and ensure that the codebase is always in a deployable state.

- **Benefits of CI**:
  - o Reduces integration problems by merging changes regularly.
  - o Encourages writing automated tests, which improves code quality.
  - o Enables quick feedback on code changes.

CI Pipeline typically involves:

1. **Code Commit**: Developers push their changes to a version control system (e.g., Git).
2. **Build**: The CI tool compiles the code and runs unit tests.
3. **Test**: Automated tests (unit tests, integration tests) are executed to ensure that changes don't break the application.
4. **Artifact Creation**: The application is packaged into deployable artifacts (e.g., Docker images, JAR files, etc.).

2. Continuous Delivery (CD)

Continuous Delivery extends CI by automating the deployment process, ensuring that the application is ready for production at any time. With CD, you can release new features to users quickly and reliably by pushing code changes to staging or production environments automatically after passing tests.

- **Benefits of CD**:
  - o Reduces the time to deliver new features.
  - o Ensures that your application is always in a deployable state.
  - o Reduces deployment risk by automating the release process.

The **CD pipeline** typically includes:

1. **Staging Deployment**: After passing the CI pipeline, the application is deployed to a staging environment that mirrors production.
2. **Production Deployment**: Once validated, the application is automatically deployed to the production environment, either manually or automatically.

3. The Importance of CI/CD

CI/CD helps organizations to:

- Improve collaboration between development and operations teams.
- Deliver features and bug fixes faster.
- Maintain high-quality code.
- Ensure that deployments are consistent and reproducible.

- Minimize human error during deployments.

Part 2: How to Implement CI/CD Pipelines Using Python, C#, and Modern DevOps Tools

1. Setting Up CI/CD for Python Projects

For Python, tools like **GitHub Actions**, **Jenkins**, **Travis CI**, and **GitLab CI/CD** are commonly used to implement CI/CD pipelines.

1.1 Setting Up a Basic CI Pipeline with GitHub Actions

GitHub Actions is a powerful CI/CD tool integrated directly with GitHub repositories. Let's create a basic pipeline for a Python project using GitHub Actions.

1. **Create a `.github/workflows/python-app.yml` file** in your repository.

```yaml
name: Python CI

on:
  push:
    branches:
      - main
  pull_request:
```

```
    branches:
      - main

jobs:
  build:
    runs-on: ubuntu-latest
    steps:
    - name: Checkout code
      uses: actions/checkout@v2
    - name: Set up Python
      uses: actions/setup-python@v2
      with:
        python-version: '3.x'
    - name: Install dependencies
      run: |
        python -m pip install --upgrade pip
        pip install -r requirements.txt
    - name: Run tests
      run: |
        pytest
```

Explanation:

- This pipeline is triggered on any push or pull request to the **main** branch.
- It sets up a Python environment, installs dependencies from `requirements.txt`, and runs tests using **pytest**.

2. **Push Code to GitHub**:

o When you push changes to the **main** branch, GitHub Actions will automatically run the pipeline, installing dependencies and running tests.

2. Setting Up CI/CD for C# Projects

For C# projects, **Azure DevOps** and **GitHub Actions** are commonly used for implementing CI/CD pipelines.

2.1 Setting Up a Basic CI/CD Pipeline with GitHub Actions for a C# Project

1. **Create a `.github/workflows/dotnet.yml` file** in your repository.

```yaml
yaml

name: .NET Core CI/CD

on:
  push:
    branches:
      - main

jobs:
  build:
    runs-on: ubuntu-latest
    steps:
```

122

```
- name: Checkout code
  uses: actions/checkout@v2
- name: Setup .NET
  uses: actions/setup-dotnet@v1
  with:
    dotnet-version: '5.x'
- name: Restore dependencies
  run: dotnet restore
- name: Build project
  run: dotnet build --configuration Release
- name: Run tests
  run: dotnet test --configuration Release
```

Explanation:

- This pipeline is triggered when there is a push to the **main** branch.

- It sets up the .NET environment, restores dependencies, builds the project, and runs unit tests.

2. **Deploy to a Web App (Azure)**: You can extend this pipeline to deploy the C# application to **Azure** or any cloud platform. Here's an example of adding deployment steps using **Azure Web Apps**.

yaml

```
- name: Deploy to Azure
  uses: Azure/webapps-deploy@v2
```

```
with:
    app-name: 'your-app-name'
    publish-profile:                    ${{
secrets.AZURE_WEBAPP_PUBLISH_PROFILE }}
    package:
$(System.DefaultWorkingDirectory)/_artifact/you
r-package.zip
```

3. Modern DevOps Tools for CI/CD Pipelines

- **Jenkins**: Jenkins is an open-source automation server widely used for CI/CD. You can create pipelines using **Jenkinsfile**, which defines the steps for build, test, and deploy processes.
- **GitLab CI/CD**: GitLab provides built-in CI/CD tools, including pipelines and runners. A `.gitlab-ci.yml` file defines the pipeline stages, similar to GitHub Actions or Jenkins.
- **Azure DevOps**: Azure DevOps provides a complete suite of tools for CI/CD. It includes **Azure Pipelines**, which support a wide range of technologies, including .NET, Java, Python, and Node.js.

Part 3: Real-World CI/CD Pipeline Example

Let's consider a real-world scenario where we have a Python application that needs to be tested and deployed.

Example: Full CI/CD Pipeline for a Python Web App

The pipeline involves:

1. **Testing** the code with **pytest**.
2. **Building** the Docker image for the application.
3. **Pushing** the Docker image to **Docker Hub**.
4. **Deploying** the Docker container to **AWS ECS** (Elastic Container Service).

GitHub Actions Workflow for Full CI/CD:

yaml

```yaml
name: Python CI/CD with Docker

on:
  push:
    branches:
      - main

jobs:
  build:
    runs-on: ubuntu-latest
    steps:
    - name: Checkout code
      uses: actions/checkout@v2

    # Set up Python environment
    - name: Set up Python
      uses: actions/setup-python@v2
```

```
with:
  python-version: '3.x'

# Install dependencies
- name: Install dependencies
  run: |
    python -m pip install --upgrade pip
    pip install -r requirements.txt

# Run tests
- name: Run tests
  run: |
    pytest

# Build Docker image
- name: Build Docker image
  run: |
    docker build -t yourdockerhub/your-image
    .

# Push Docker image to Docker Hub
- name: Push Docker image to Docker Hub
  run: |
    docker login -u ${{
secrets.DOCKER_USERNAME }} -p ${{
secrets.DOCKER_PASSWORD }}
    docker push yourdockerhub/your-image

deploy:
```

```
runs-on: ubuntu-latest
needs: build
steps:
- name: Deploy to AWS ECS
  run: |
      ecs-cli configure --region us-west-2 --
access-key-id ${{ secrets.AWS_ACCESS_KEY_ID }} -
-secret-access-key                         ${{
secrets.AWS_SECRET_ACCESS_KEY }} --cluster your-
cluster-name
      ecs-cli    compose    --file    docker-
compose.yml up
```

Explanation:

- **Build and Test**: The pipeline installs dependencies, runs tests, and builds the Docker image.
- **Push to Docker Hub**: The Docker image is pushed to Docker Hub using credentials stored in GitHub secrets.
- **Deploy to AWS ECS**: Once the image is pushed, it is deployed to **AWS ECS** for production deployment.

This pipeline automates testing, building, and deployment, ensuring that your Python web application is continuously integrated and delivered to production with minimal manual intervention.

Conclusion

In this chapter, we explored **Continuous Integration (CI)** and **Continuous Delivery (CD)** concepts and their importance in modern DevOps practices. We discussed how to set up CI/CD pipelines using **Python** and **C#** with tools like **GitHub Actions** and **Azure DevOps**. We also looked at a real-world example of a full CI/CD pipeline for a Python web app, covering testing, building, pushing to Docker Hub, and deploying to **AWS ECS**. By implementing CI/CD, you can automate your software delivery process, ensure high-quality code, and streamline the deployment of applications across multiple platforms.

CHAPTER 12

TESTING AND DEBUGGING CROSS-PLATFORM APPLICATIONS

Testing and debugging are crucial steps in the software development lifecycle, especially when building cross-platform applications. These processes help ensure that your app performs as expected on different devices and platforms. In this chapter, we will explore how to test applications on multiple platforms, discuss debugging techniques specific to **Python** and **C#**, and walk through a real-world debugging scenario and how to resolve issues.

Part 1: How to Test Your Applications on Multiple Platforms

Cross-platform applications often need to be tested on multiple operating systems and devices. Testing on different platforms ensures that your app behaves consistently and meets platform-specific expectations.

1. Manual Testing Across Platforms

Manual testing involves running the application on different platforms (Windows, macOS, Linux, Android, iOS) to check for compatibility and functionality.

- **Desktop Testing**: For desktop applications, you can install your app on **Windows**, **macOS**, and **Linux**. You can either set up different physical machines or use virtual machines (VMs) to run each platform.
- **Mobile Testing**: For mobile apps, you can test on **Android** and **iOS** devices or use simulators/emulators. Tools like **Xcode** for iOS and **Android Studio** for Android offer emulators to simulate different device types.

2. Automated Testing Across Platforms

Automated testing is essential for maintaining code quality in cross-platform development. It allows you to run tests on multiple platforms without manual intervention, which saves time and ensures consistency.

For Python:

- **PyTest**: A popular testing framework for Python that supports cross-platform testing. PyTest can be used to run unit tests, integration tests, and functional tests on different platforms.

- **Appium**: For mobile app testing, **Appium** allows you to write automated tests for iOS and Android apps using a single test script.

For C#:

- **NUnit**: A popular testing framework for C# that supports unit testing and integration testing. It can be used in combination with CI tools to test applications on various platforms.
- **Xamarin.UITest**: For testing Xamarin mobile apps, **Xamarin.UITest** allows you to write cross-platform UI tests for Android and iOS apps.

3. Cross-Platform Testing Frameworks

Some frameworks make it easier to run tests on multiple platforms without writing separate tests for each platform.

- **Appium**: An open-source framework that allows you to run cross-platform mobile tests on both **iOS** and **Android**.
- **Selenium**: Although traditionally used for web applications, **Selenium** can be used for automated

browser testing on different operating systems (Windows, macOS, Linux).

4. Cloud-based Testing Tools

Cloud services like **BrowserStack** and **Sauce Labs** provide access to real devices and browsers for testing. These services allow you to run tests on real hardware without needing to maintain multiple devices or environments yourself.

- **BrowserStack**: Supports cross-browser testing for web apps across various operating systems and devices.
- **Sauce Labs**: Provides real-device testing for mobile applications, including Android and iOS.

Part 2: Debugging Techniques Specific to Python and C#

Debugging is a crucial part of development, especially when working with cross-platform apps. Effective debugging tools and techniques can save you a lot of time and effort in diagnosing and fixing issues.

1. Debugging in Python

Python provides various tools for debugging, from simple print statements to more advanced debuggers.

1.1   Using   Print   Statements

A common debugging technique is to add print statements to your code to output values and check the flow of execution.

python

```python
def add_numbers(a, b):
    print(f"Adding {a} and {b}")   # Debugging output
    return a + b

result = add_numbers(5, 10)
print(f"Result: {result}")
```

1.2   Using   pdb   (Python   Debugger)

For more advanced debugging, Python includes the built-in pdb module, which allows you to set breakpoints and step through your code.

python

```python
import pdb

def add_numbers(a, b):
    pdb.set_trace()   # Set a breakpoint
    return a + b

result = add_numbers(5, 10)
```

When the code hits the `set_trace()` line, the debugger will pause, and you can inspect variables, step through the code, and continue execution interactively.

1.3 Using IDE Debugger (e.g., PyCharm, VSCode)
Most Python IDEs, like **PyCharm** or **VSCode**, have built-in debuggers that offer a GUI for setting breakpoints, inspecting variables, and stepping through code.

2. Debugging in C#

In C#, debugging is typically done using **Visual Studio** or **Visual Studio Code** with the C# extension.

2.1   Using   Breakpoints
In Visual Studio, you can set breakpoints by clicking on the left margin next to the line of code where you want to pause execution. Once the breakpoint is hit, you can inspect variables and step through the code.

```csharp
class Program
{
    static void Main()
    {
        int result = AddNumbers(5, 10);
```

```csharp
        Console.WriteLine($"Result: {result}");
    }

    static int AddNumbers(int a, int b)
    {
        int sum = a + b;
        return sum;
    }
}
```

2.2   Using   `Debug.WriteLine()`

You can use `Debug.WriteLine()` to output messages to the
Output window in Visual Studio for debugging purposes.

csharp

```csharp
using System.Diagnostics;

class Program
{
    static void Main()
    {
        Debug.WriteLine("Starting
application...");
        int result = AddNumbers(5, 10);
        Debug.WriteLine($"Result: {result}");
    }

    static int AddNumbers(int a, int b)
```

```
{
    return a + b;
}
}
```

2.3 Debugging in Visual Studio Code

Visual Studio Code supports debugging through the **C# extension**. You can set breakpoints, step through code, and inspect variables similarly to Visual Studio, but it works across multiple platforms, including **Windows, macOS**, and **Linux**.

3. Cross-Platform Debugging Tools

For cross-platform debugging, some tools can be used to debug both Python and C# applications on different platforms.

- **Visual Studio Code**: Offers debugging support for both **Python** (via the Python extension) and **C#** (via the C# extension).
- **Xamarin Live Reload**: If you are using Xamarin for mobile app development, **Xamarin Live Reload** allows you to instantly see changes to your app on Android and iOS devices without rebuilding the app.

Part 3: Real-World Debugging Scenario and How to Resolve Issues

Let's walk through a real-world debugging scenario where we have an issue in both Python and C# applications.

1. Python Debugging Scenario

Problem: You have a Python app that reads data from a file and processes it, but the program crashes with an error when trying to read the file.

Steps to Debug:

1. Use `print()` statements to check if the file path is correct.
2. Use `pdb` to step through the code and identify the point of failure.
3. Check if the file exists and ensure you are opening it correctly.

Python Code:

```python
python


import pdb
import os

def read_file(file_path):
```

```
pdb.set_trace()   # Start debugging here
if not os.path.exists(file_path):
    print("File does not exist")
    return None
with open(file_path, 'r') as file:
    data = file.read()
return data


result = read_file('data.txt')
print(f"File Content: {result}")
```

Resolution: After debugging, you find that the file path is incorrect. You update the path to the correct location, and the program runs as expected.

2. C# Debugging Scenario

Problem: Your C# application is returning an incorrect result from a method that calculates the total of an order, and the total is always zero.

Steps to Debug:

1. Set a breakpoint at the method where the total is calculated.
2. Step through the code to inspect the variables and identify any incorrect logic or values.
3. Verify if the correct data is being passed into the method.

138

C# Code:

```
csharp

using System;

class Program
{
    static void Main()
    {
        int total = CalculateOrderTotal(5, 10);
        Console.WriteLine($"Order        Total:
{total}");
    }

    static int CalculateOrderTotal(int price,
int quantity)
    {
        int total = price * quantity;
        return total;
    }
}
```

Resolution: Upon inspection, you discover that the method was working fine, but you were passing in incorrect values to the function in the main program. After updating the values, the total is calculated correctly.

Conclusion

In this chapter, we covered the essential aspects of **testing** and **debugging** cross-platform applications. We discussed various techniques for testing across platforms, using both **manual** and **automated testing** methods. We also explored debugging techniques specific to **Python** and **C#**, highlighting tools such as `pdb`, Visual Studio, and breakpoints. Finally, we walked through a real-world debugging scenario and the steps to resolve issues in both Python and C# applications. By following these strategies, you can ensure that your cross-platform applications are robust, reliable, and free of critical issues.

CHAPTER 13

CLOUD INTEGRATION: BRINGING YOUR APP TO THE CLOUD

Cloud computing has revolutionized the way applications are developed, deployed, and scaled. For cross-platform apps, integrating with cloud services is critical for enabling features like real-time data synchronization, scalability, and easy access to resources. This chapter will introduce cloud computing and its significance for cross-platform apps, guide you through setting up cloud services for **Python** and **C#** applications, and demonstrate how to deploy a basic app to the cloud.

Part 1: Introduction to Cloud Computing and Why It's Important for Cross-Platform Apps

1. What is Cloud Computing?

Cloud computing refers to the delivery of computing services (such as servers, storage, databases, networking, software, and more) over the internet (the cloud) instead of using local servers or personal devices. It allows developers to rent computing resources on-demand, enabling scalable and flexible solutions without having to manage hardware infrastructure.

There are three primary models of cloud computing:

- **IaaS (Infrastructure as a Service)**: Provides virtualized computing resources over the internet (e.g., AWS EC2, Microsoft Azure Virtual Machines).
- **PaaS (Platform as a Service)**: Provides a platform allowing customers to develop, run, and manage applications without dealing with infrastructure (e.g., AWS Elastic Beanstalk, Azure App Services).
- **SaaS (Software as a Service)**: Provides access to software applications hosted in the cloud (e.g., Google Docs, Salesforce).

2. Why is Cloud Integration Important for Cross-Platform Apps?

For cross-platform applications, cloud services provide several advantages:

- **Scalability**: Cloud platforms automatically scale resources based on usage, ensuring that the application can handle increased load efficiently.
- **Data Synchronization**: Cloud storage allows you to synchronize data across different devices, ensuring that

users have consistent access to their data, regardless of the platform.

- **Remote Access and Collaboration**: Cloud computing enables teams to collaborate and access applications from anywhere, providing flexibility and improving productivity.
- **Cost Efficiency**: Cloud services are often more affordable than maintaining physical infrastructure, as you only pay for the resources you use.
- **Security**: Cloud providers implement robust security measures, including encryption, backup, and compliance with industry standards.

By integrating your cross-platform app with the cloud, you can leverage these benefits to enhance the app's functionality, user experience, and performance.

Part 2: Setting Up Cloud Services (AWS, Azure) for Python and C# Apps

1. Setting Up AWS for Python Apps

Amazon Web Services (AWS) offers a wide range of services for app deployment, including **EC2** (Elastic Compute Cloud), **S3** (Simple Storage Service), and **Elastic Beanstalk** for web application deployment.

1.1 Setting Up AWS for Python Apps with Elastic Beanstalk Elastic Beanstalk is a **PaaS** offering from AWS that allows you to deploy and manage Python applications without needing to manage the underlying infrastructure.

Steps to Deploy a Python App to AWS Elastic Beanstalk:

1. **Install AWS CLI**:
   - To interact with AWS, you need to install and configure the **AWS CLI** (Command Line Interface).

```bash
pip install awscli
aws configure
```

During configuration, provide your AWS access key, secret key, region, and output format.

2. **Create an Elastic Beanstalk Application**:
   - Create a Python web application, for example, using **Flask**.

```python
from flask import Flask
app = Flask(__name__)
```

144

```
@app.route('/')
def hello():
    return 'Hello, World!'


if __name__ == '__main__':
    app.run(debug=True)
```

3. **Prepare Your Application for Deployment**:
   - o Create a `requirements.txt` file listing the dependencies.

```bash
```

```
flask
```

   - o Include a **Procfile** to specify the start command for your app.

```text
```

```
web: python application.py
```

4. **Deploy to Elastic Beanstalk**:
   - o Initialize your Elastic Beanstalk environment.

```bash
```

```
eb init -p python-3.x my-python-app
```

145

```
eb create my-python-app-env
eb deploy
```

5. **Access Your Application**:
   o Once deployed, you can access your app via the URL provided by AWS Elastic Beanstalk.

2. Setting Up Azure for C# Apps

Microsoft Azure is a cloud platform offering a variety of services for C# applications, including **App Services** for web apps, **Azure Functions** for serverless computing, and **Azure Blob Storage** for file storage.

2.1 Setting Up Azure for C# Web Apps with Azure App Services Azure App Services is a fully managed **PaaS** offering for building, deploying, and scaling web apps. Here's how to deploy a C# web application to Azure.

Steps to Deploy a C# Web App to Azure App Services:

1. **Create a C# Web App**:
   o Create a simple ASP.NET Core web application using **Visual Studio** or **Visual Studio Code**.

```csharp
using Microsoft.AspNetCore.Mvc;
```

```
namespace HelloWorldApp.Controllers
{
    [Route("api/[controller]")]
    [ApiController]
    public    class    HelloController    :
ControllerBase
    {
        [HttpGet]
        public IActionResult Get()
        {
            return Ok("Hello, World!");
        }
    }
}
```

2. **Install Azure CLI**:

   o Download and install the **Azure CLI** for managing Azure resources from the command line.

```bash
bash
```

```
curl -sL https://aka.ms/InstallAzureCLIDeb
| sudo bash
```

3. **Create and Deploy Your Web App to Azure**:

   o Login to Azure using the CLI.

```
bash
```

```
az login
```

- o Create a new web app in Azure.

```
bash
```

```
az webapp up --name my-csharp-webapp --
resource-group    myResourceGroup    --plan
myAppServicePlan
```

4. **Access Your Web App**:
   - o Once deployed, you can access your app through the provided Azure URL.

Part 3: Real-World Example: Deploying a Basic App to the Cloud

Let's deploy a simple Python web application to AWS and a C# application to Azure, demonstrating the deployment process for both cloud platforms.

1. Python Example: Deploying a Flask App to AWS

1. **Application**: A simple Flask web app that returns "Hello, World!" when accessed.
2. **Setup**: We used **Elastic Beanstalk** in AWS for the deployment.
3. **Deployment**:

- o First, we packaged the app with necessary dependencies (`requirements.txt`, `Procfile`).
- o Then, using the AWS CLI, we initialized the application and deployed it using `eb deploy`.

4. **Result**: The app is now accessible via an AWS-provided URL, and it is ready to scale automatically based on demand.

2. C# Example: Deploying an ASP.NET Core App to Azure

1. **Application**: A simple ASP.NET Core web API that returns "Hello, World!".
2. **Setup**: We used **Azure App Services** for deployment.
3. **Deployment**:
   - o We created the application in **Visual Studio** and then deployed it using the **Azure CLI**.
4. **Result**: The app is now running in Azure App Services and accessible via an Azure-provided URL. Azure automatically handles scaling based on demand.

Conclusion

In this chapter, we explored **cloud integration** for cross-platform applications. We introduced the concept of cloud computing and highlighted its importance in enabling cross-platform apps to scale, synchronize data, and take advantage

149

of cloud resources. We discussed how to set up cloud services like **AWS** and **Azure** for **Python** and **C#** applications, respectively. Finally, we walked through real-world examples of deploying a basic Flask app to AWS and a simple ASP.NET Core app to Azure, demonstrating how cloud services simplify deployment and scaling. By integrating cloud services, cross-platform apps can leverage the power of cloud computing to offer better performance, security, and user experience.

CHAPTER 14

PERFORMANCE OPTIMIZATION ACROSS PLATFORMS

Performance is one of the most critical factors that affect the user experience of an application. For cross-platform apps, it's essential to ensure that the application runs smoothly across all target platforms, whether it's **mobile** (iOS, Android) or **desktop** (Windows, macOS, Linux). In this chapter, we will discuss strategies for optimizing performance, including techniques specific to both mobile and desktop platforms, and share real-world performance testing and optimization examples.

Part 1: How to Ensure Your App Performs Well on All Platforms

When building a cross-platform app, the goal is to maintain consistent performance across different devices and operating systems. This involves optimizing the app's **speed**, **responsiveness**, and **resource consumption** to create a seamless experience for users.

1. Identify Platform-Specific Performance Bottlenecks

Different platforms can have unique performance characteristics. For example, mobile devices typically have fewer resources (like RAM and processing power) compared to desktop devices. Similarly, **iOS** and **Android** have different behaviors in terms of resource management, so it's important to optimize your app for both.

- **Mobile**: Mobile apps typically need to manage battery life, processing power, and memory efficiently. Performance bottlenecks on mobile devices often occur due to inefficient rendering, excessive memory use, or network requests.

- **Desktop**: Desktop apps have more processing power and memory but might encounter performance issues due to heavy resource consumption or poorly optimized UI components.

2. General Best Practices for Cross-Platform Performance

Regardless of the platform, there are several best practices you can follow to optimize your app's performance:

- **Minimize Main Thread Usage**: Ensure that the main thread isn't blocked by heavy tasks like database queries, network requests, or large computations. Offload such tasks to background threads or use asynchronous operations.

- **Optimize Memory Usage**: Avoid memory leaks by carefully managing object references and deallocating memory when no longer needed.

- **Reduce Redundant Operations**: Repeatedly executing the same tasks (like fetching the same data) can degrade performance. Cache results where appropriate and minimize redundant operations.

- **Efficient Data Handling**: Handle large data sets efficiently by using techniques like pagination, lazy loading, or background data synchronization.

3. Cross-Platform Tools for Performance Profiling

There are various tools and libraries available to help you profile and monitor your app's performance across platforms:

- **Xamarin Profiler**: For Xamarin apps, this tool provides insights into memory usage, CPU usage, and network requests, helping you identify performance bottlenecks.

- **Py-Spy**: For Python applications, **Py-Spy** is a sampling profiler that can be used to monitor CPU usage and identify slow functions.

- **Chrome DevTools**: For web apps, Chrome DevTools allows you to profile JavaScript performance, network usage, and rendering performance.
- **Visual Studio Profiler**: For C# applications, the **Visual Studio Profiler** provides tools for analyzing CPU usage, memory consumption, and thread activity.

Part 2: Optimizing for Mobile and Desktop Platforms

1. Optimizing for Mobile Platforms

Optimizing for mobile devices is essential due to the constraints on CPU, memory, and battery life.

- **Reduce Battery Consumption**: Mobile apps should minimize background processes, limit unnecessary sensor usage (like GPS), and optimize network requests.
    - Use **background threads** to handle tasks that don't need immediate user interaction, and limit the use of location services or push notifications to prevent excessive battery drain.
- **Optimize UI Rendering**: Avoid over-rendering views, which can be a common cause of UI lag on mobile devices.

- Use **View Recycling** (for example, **RecyclerView** on Android) to efficiently reuse views when scrolling through lists.
- **Lazy load** images and assets to reduce initial load times.

- **Efficient Networking**: Network requests on mobile can be slower due to less reliable internet connections. Use **HTTP caching, compression**, and **image optimization** to minimize the amount of data transferred.
  - Use libraries like **Retrofit** (Android) or **Alamofire** (iOS) to simplify network requests and manage retries and timeouts.

- **Optimize Memory Usage**: Mobile devices have limited memory. Use tools like **Xcode Instruments** (iOS) and **Android Profiler** to monitor memory consumption and identify leaks or excessive memory usage.

2. Optimizing for Desktop Platforms

Desktop apps have more resources, but they also face performance challenges, such as handling large datasets or processing-intensive tasks.

155

- **Efficient Resource Management**: Use memory efficiently by releasing resources (e.g., database connections, file handles) when they are no longer needed. Be mindful of background processes consuming too much CPU power.

- **GPU Acceleration**: Take advantage of GPU acceleration for rendering and processing graphics-intensive tasks. Use libraries like **OpenGL** (cross-platform) or platform-specific libraries like **DirectX** (Windows) and **Metal** (macOS).

- **Multithreading and Parallelism**: Desktop apps can benefit significantly from parallel processing to speed up data processing. Use **Task Parallel Library (TPL)** in C# or Python's **concurrent.futures** module to divide tasks into smaller, parallelizable chunks.

- **Optimize Startup Time**: Desktop applications should start quickly. Minimize the work done during startup by deferring non-essential tasks or lazy-loading components.

Part 3: Real-World Performance Testing and Optimization Techniques

1. Performance Testing Example for a Python App

Let's consider a **Python web app** that performs data processing and returns results via an API.

Problem: The app is slow when processing large datasets.

Testing the App's Performance:

1. Use **cProfile** to profile the performance of the Python app and identify slow functions.

   bash

   ```
   python -m cProfile -s time app.py
   ```

2. Use **Py-Spy** to visualize where the application spends most of its time.

   bash

   ```
   py-spy top --pid <your_pid>
   ```

Optimization:

1. **Database Query Optimization**: If the app performs inefficient database queries, optimize them by indexing frequently queried columns and using pagination for large data sets.

2. **Parallel Processing**: If data processing is CPU-bound, use **concurrent.futures** or **multiprocessing** to parallelize the work.

   python

   ```python
   from concurrent.futures import ProcessPoolExecutor

   def process_data(data):
       # Processing logic here
       return processed_data

   with ProcessPoolExecutor() as executor:
       results = list(executor.map(process_data, large_data_set))
   ```

3. **Caching Results**: If the app repeatedly fetches the same data, implement caching using libraries like **joblib** or **Flask-Caching** to speed up subsequent requests.

2. Performance Testing Example for a C# App

Let's consider a **C# desktop app** that processes large files and displays the results in a UI.

Problem: The app has a noticeable delay when opening large files.

Testing the App's Performance:

1. Use **Visual Studio Profiler** to monitor CPU and memory usage during file opening.
2. Use **BenchmarkDotNet** to run benchmarks on different parts of the application to pinpoint the slowest parts.

Optimization:

1. **Async File Handling**: For large files, use asynchronous methods to prevent blocking the UI thread.

```csharp
using System.IO;
using System.Threading.Tasks;

public        async        Task<string>
ReadFileAsync(string filePath)
```

159

```
{
    using (StreamReader reader = new
StreamReader(filePath))
    {
        return                  await
reader.ReadToEndAsync();
    }
}
```

2. **Efficient File Parsing**: Use **streaming** techniques to process files line-by-line instead of reading them entirely into memory.

csharp

```
foreach (var line in
File.ReadLines(filePath))
{
    // Process each line
}
```

3. **Optimize UI Rendering**: If UI rendering is slow due to processing, use **background workers** or **Task.Run** to offload processing tasks from the main UI thread.

3. Cross-Platform Performance Testing with Xamarin

Let's consider a **Xamarin mobile app** that retrieves and displays a list of products from a remote server.

Problem: The list of products loads slowly on both iOS and Android.

Testing the App's Performance:

1. Use **Xamarin Profiler** to analyze CPU usage, memory consumption, and network latency.
2. Use **Xamarin Insights** or **App Center** to monitor app performance in real-time across different devices.

Optimization:

1. **Lazy Loading**: Implement **pagination** or **lazy loading** to only fetch a small number of items initially and load more as the user scrolls.
2. **Network Request Optimization**: Use **compression** and **HTTP caching** to reduce the data transferred and speed up the response time.
3. **Asynchronous Programming**: Ensure that all network requests and long-running tasks are handled asynchronously using **async/await** to keep the UI responsive.

161

Conclusion

In this chapter, we explored **performance optimization** strategies for cross-platform applications. We discussed general best practices for ensuring optimal performance across platforms, specific optimizations for **mobile** and **desktop** platforms, and real-world performance testing and optimization techniques. Whether you are working with a **Python web app**, **C# desktop app**, or **Xamarin mobile app**, the key to optimizing performance lies in identifying bottlenecks, improving efficiency, and using platform-specific tools to monitor and adjust resource usage. By following these strategies, you can ensure that your cross-platform app performs smoothly and delivers an excellent user experience.

CHAPTER 15

DEVOPS AND AUTOMATION: STREAMLINING DEVELOPMENT

DevOps is a set of practices and tools that integrate software development (Dev) and IT operations (Ops) to shorten the development lifecycle and deliver high-quality software continuously. Automation is a key aspect of DevOps, allowing teams to streamline their workflows, reduce human error, and increase productivity. This chapter will explore the role of **DevOps** in cross-platform development, how to automate repetitive tasks using **DevOps tools** like **Docker** and **Kubernetes**, and present real-world examples of automation pipelines to enhance your development process.

Part 1: The Role of DevOps in Cross-Platform Development

DevOps plays a crucial role in cross-platform development by enabling teams to deliver software faster, with greater reliability, and across multiple platforms (e.g., mobile, desktop, and cloud environments). With the variety of platforms and environments that cross-platform applications must support, DevOps practices provide a framework for managing complexity and ensuring consistency.

1. Benefits of DevOps for Cross-Platform Apps

- **Faster Time to Market**: DevOps emphasizes automation and continuous integration (CI), allowing development teams to build, test, and deploy applications rapidly and reliably across all platforms.
- **Consistency Across Environments**: DevOps ensures that the software works the same way on every platform by using automation tools like Docker to create consistent development, staging, and production environments.
- **Improved Collaboration**: By breaking down silos between developers, operations, and quality assurance teams, DevOps fosters better communication and collaboration, leading to smoother development cycles.
- **Scalability**: With DevOps tools like Kubernetes, you can automate scaling and deployment to handle increased traffic across multiple platforms, ensuring that your app performs well under load.

2. Key DevOps Concepts for Cross-Platform Development

- **Continuous Integration (CI)**: CI automates the integration of new code changes into the shared repository. This practice reduces integration problems and helps detect issues early, making it a critical component of cross-platform development.

- **Continuous Delivery (CD)**: CD automates the deployment of applications to different environments, ensuring that code changes are automatically tested and released in a consistent manner across platforms.

- **Infrastructure as Code (IaC)**: IaC allows you to define and manage infrastructure using code, making it easier to set up and maintain environments for multiple platforms.

- **Monitoring and Logging**: DevOps tools help you monitor the performance of your app on multiple platforms, providing valuable insights into user behavior and system health.

Part 2: How to Automate Repetitive Tasks with DevOps Tools

1. Docker: Containerizing Applications for Consistency Across Platforms

Docker is a platform for developing, shipping, and running applications inside containers. Containers package an application with everything it needs (e.g., libraries, dependencies, configurations) and ensure it runs consistently on any system, whether it's **Windows, macOS**, or **Linux**.

1.1 Using Docker to Automate Cross-Platform Deployment

With Docker, you can automate the process of building, testing, and deploying applications across platforms by ensuring that they run the same way in different environments.

Example: Dockerizing a Python Web App

1. **Create a `Dockerfile` for the Python app**:
   - o A Dockerfile is a script containing instructions on how to build a Docker image for your application.

   ```
   Dockerfile

   # Use an official Python runtime as a
   parent image
   FROM python:3.9-slim

   # Set the working directory in the
   container
   WORKDIR /app

   # the current directory contents into the
   container at /app
     . /app
   ```

166

```
# Install any needed packages specified in
requirements.txt
RUN   pip   install   --no-cache-dir   -r
requirements.txt

# Make port 5000 available to the world
outside the container
EXPOSE 5000

# Run the application
CMD ["python", "app.py"]
```

2. **Build the Docker image**:

```bash
docker build -t my-python-app .
```

3. **Run the Docker container**:

```bash
docker run -p 5000:5000 my-python-app
```

This Docker container ensures that the Python app behaves consistently regardless of the host environment, making it easier to deploy the app on **Windows, Linux,** or **macOS**.

1.2 Automating Docker Builds with CI Tools

You can automate the Docker build and deployment process using CI tools like **Jenkins**, **GitHub Actions**, or **GitLab CI/CD**. For example, using GitHub Actions:

```yaml
yaml

name: Docker Build and Deploy

on:
  push:
    branches:
      - main

jobs:
  build:
    runs-on: ubuntu-latest
    steps:
    - name: Checkout code
      uses: actions/checkout@v2
    - name: Set up Docker Buildx
      uses: docker/setup-buildx-action@v1
    - name: Cache Docker layers
      uses: actions/cache@v2
      with:
        path: /tmp/.buildx-cache
        key: ${{ runner.os }}-buildx-${{ github.sha }}
```

```
- name: Build and push Docker image
  run: |
      docker build -t my-python-app .
      docker push my-python-app
```

This YAML configuration builds the Docker image automatically whenever changes are pushed to the **main** branch and pushes it to a Docker registry (e.g., Docker Hub).

2. Kubernetes: Automating Deployment and Scaling

Kubernetes is an open-source platform that automates container orchestration, deployment, scaling, and management. For cross-platform applications, Kubernetes can manage the deployment and scaling of containers across different environments and platforms, ensuring high availability and efficient resource utilization.

2.1 Automating Deployment with Kubernetes

Kubernetes helps automate the deployment and scaling of applications by managing a cluster of machines (nodes) that run containers.

Example: Deploying a Dockerized App to Kubernetes

1. **Create a Kubernetes Deployment configuration** (in a file named `deployment.yaml`):

yaml

```yaml
apiVersion: apps/v1
kind: Deployment
metadata:
  name: my-python-app
spec:
  replicas: 3
  selector:
    matchLabels:
      app: my-python-app
  template:
    metadata:
      labels:
        app: my-python-app
    spec:
      containers:
      - name: my-python-app
        image: my-python-app
        ports:
        - containerPort: 5000
```

2. **Apply the deployment to the Kubernetes cluster:**

bash

```
kubectl apply -f deployment.yaml
```

3. **Expose the app using a Kubernetes Service**:

```yaml
yaml

apiVersion: v1
kind: Service
metadata:
  name: my-python-app-service
spec:
  selector:
    app: my-python-app
  ports:
    - protocol: TCP
      port: 80
      targetPort: 5000
  type: LoadBalancer
```

4. **Apply the service**:

```bash
bash

kubectl apply -f service.yaml
```

Kubernetes will automatically manage scaling (adjusting the number of app replicas), handle rolling updates, and ensure high availability.

3. Automating with Other DevOps Tools

- **Jenkins**: Jenkins is an automation server that can be used to automate tasks such as building, testing, and deploying your app. Jenkins integrates with Docker and Kubernetes to create robust CI/CD pipelines.
- **GitLab CI/CD**: GitLab offers built-in support for continuous integration and deployment, including Docker and Kubernetes integration.
- **Terraform**: For Infrastructure as Code (IaC), **Terraform** helps automate the creation and management of cloud infrastructure, ensuring consistent environments for your applications.

Part 3: Real-World Example: Automation Pipelines for Cross-Platform Apps

Let's consider a cross-platform mobile app built with **Xamarin** and a Python API. We'll set up an automated CI/CD pipeline using **GitHub Actions**, **Docker**, and **Kubernetes** for deployment.

1. Automating the Xamarin App Build with GitHub Actions

We can automate the Xamarin app build and deployment process with GitHub Actions.

```yaml
yaml

name: Xamarin CI/CD

on:
  push:
    branches:
      - main

jobs:
  build:
    runs-on: ubuntu-latest
    steps:
    - name: Checkout code
      uses: actions/checkout@v2
    - name: Set up Xamarin
      uses: actions/setup-dotnet@v1
      with:
        dotnet-version: '5.x'
    - name: Restore dependencies
      run: dotnet restore
    - name: Build project
      run: dotnet build --configuration Release
    - name: Run tests
      run: dotnet test --configuration Release
    - name: Build Docker Image
      run: |
        docker build -t xamarin-app .
    - name: Deploy to Kubernetes
```

173

```
run: |
    kubectl apply -f deployment.yaml
```

This pipeline automatically builds the Xamarin app, runs tests, creates a Docker image, and deploys it to a Kubernetes cluster.

2. Deploying the Python API to the Cloud with Docker and Kubernetes

For a Python API, we can automate the Docker build and Kubernetes deployment.

1. **Build the Docker image** and **push it to Docker Hub** automatically using GitHub Actions.
2. **Deploy the app** to a Kubernetes cluster hosted on **Google Cloud** or **AWS** using `kubectl`.

```yaml
yaml

name: Python API CI/CD

on:
  push:
    branches:
      - main

jobs:
```

```
build:
  runs-on: ubuntu-latest
  steps:
  - name: Checkout code
    uses: actions/checkout@v2
  - name: Set up Python
    uses: actions/setup-python@v2
    with:
      python-version: '3.x'
  - name: Install dependencies
    run: |
      pip install -r requirements.txt
  - name: Build Docker image
    run: |
      docker build -t python-api .
  - name: Push Docker image to Docker Hub
    run: |
      docker login -u ${{
secrets.DOCKER_USERNAME }} -p ${{
secrets.DOCKER_PASSWORD }}
      docker push python-api
  - name: Deploy to Kubernetes
    run: |
      kubectl apply -f deployment.yaml
```

Conclusion

In this chapter, we explored the role of **DevOps** in cross-platform development, focusing on how it streamlines development through automation. We discussed tools like

Docker and **Kubernetes**, which enable developers to automate repetitive tasks such as building, testing, and deploying applications. Through real-world examples, we demonstrated how to set up CI/CD pipelines for both **Xamarin** and **Python** apps, automating the process of building, testing, and deploying code. By integrating **DevOps practices**, you can optimize your development workflow, ensure consistency across platforms, and reduce manual intervention, enabling faster and more reliable software delivery.

CHAPTER 16

MONITORING AND MAINTAINING CROSS-PLATFORM APPLICATIONS

Once your cross-platform application is live, the work doesn't stop there. Ongoing **monitoring**, **maintenance**, and **updates** are crucial to ensure that your app performs optimally across all platforms, providing users with a seamless experience. This chapter will discuss how to set up monitoring tools, the importance of keeping your app updated across platforms, and provide a real-world example of how to monitor an app post-launch.

Part 1: Setting Up Monitoring Tools for Your Apps

Monitoring is a continuous process that helps you track your app's performance, detect potential issues, and optimize the user experience. For cross-platform applications, setting up robust monitoring tools is essential to track application health, errors, and user behavior across all platforms (e.g., mobile, desktop, web).

1. Popular Monitoring Tools

There are several popular tools that provide comprehensive monitoring capabilities for cross-platform applications, from **error tracking** and **performance monitoring** to **real-time application performance management (APM)**.

1.1 Datadog

Datadog is a cloud-based monitoring and analytics platform that provides a wide range of monitoring capabilities for cross-platform applications. It helps track application performance, infrastructure metrics, logs, and errors, all in real time.

- **Features**:
  - **APM (Application Performance Monitoring)**: Tracks the performance of your application, including response times, error rates, and throughput.
  - **Real-Time Dashboards**: Visualize data from various sources to monitor your app's performance in real-time.
  - **Error Tracking**: Track application errors and bugs across platforms.

o **Integration**: Datadog integrates with various services like AWS, Azure, Docker, Kubernetes, and more, providing unified monitoring for all aspects of your app.

1.2 Prometheus and Grafana

Prometheus is an open-source monitoring tool often used with **Grafana** for data visualization. It's particularly well-suited for tracking metrics and logs in real-time, making it ideal for monitoring containerized and microservice-based applications.

- **Prometheus** collects and stores metrics as time-series data.
- **Grafana** provides powerful visualizations of Prometheus data, making it easy to create custom dashboards to monitor your application's health across platforms.

1.3 Sentry

Sentry is an open-source error tracking tool that provides real-time error monitoring and debugging for applications across various platforms, including **mobile**, **web**, and **desktop**. It integrates with multiple programming languages like **JavaScript**, **Python**, **Java**, and **C#**.

- **Features**:
  - ○ **Real-Time Error Tracking**: Capture and report errors in real-time across different platforms.
  - ○ **Crash Reporting**: Track crashes and exceptions, including stack traces and user context.
  - ○ **Integration with CI/CD**: Sentry integrates seamlessly with your CI/CD pipeline, ensuring you catch issues before they reach production.

1.4 Setting Up Datadog for Cross-Platform Monitoring

Let's walk through setting up **Datadog** to monitor an app.

1. **Install Datadog Agent**:
   - ○ First, install the Datadog agent on your infrastructure. The agent collects data from various sources (servers, containers, cloud services).
   - ○ Follow the installation guide on Datadog's website for your platform.

2. **Integrating Datadog with Your Application**:
   - ○ For **Python** applications, install the Datadog APM library:

   bash

   ```
   pip install ddtrace
   ```

- o For **C#** applications, integrate the **Datadog .NET APM** library.

3. **Configure Datadog in Your Application**:

- o For Python:

```python

from ddtrace import patch_all
patch_all()

# Your application code
```

- o For C#: In your **Startup.cs** file, configure Datadog monitoring:

```csharp

public                              void
ConfigureServices(IServiceCollectio
n services)
{
    services.AddDatadogTracing();
}
```

4. **Monitor Metrics**:

- o After integrating Datadog into your app, you can view performance metrics (e.g., request latency, error rates) on your Datadog dashboard. This provides you with visibility into how your app is performing on each platform (mobile, desktop, web).

1.5 Setting Up Prometheus and Grafana

1. **Install Prometheus**:
   o Prometheus can be installed using **Docker** or directly on your server.

   bash

   ```
   docker run -d -p 9090:9090 prom/prometheus
   ```

2. **Configure Your Application to Expose Metrics**:
   o For Python, you can use **Prometheus Client** to expose metrics.

   bash

   ```
   pip install prometheus_client
   ```

   o Example:

   python

   ```
   from prometheus_client import start_http_server, Counter
   ```

```
c    =    Counter('my_app_requests',
'Total number of requests')

def increment():
    c.inc()

if __name__ == "__main__":
    start_http_server(8000)        #
Exposes metrics on port 8000
    while True:
        increment()
```

3. **Install Grafana**:

   o   Grafana is used to visualize the metrics collected by Prometheus. You can install it using Docker or directly on your server.

```bash
bash
```

```
docker run -d -p 3000:3000 grafana/grafana
```

4. **Create Dashboards in Grafana**:

   o   Once Grafana is set up, you can create dashboards that visualize metrics such as request rates, response times, error counts, etc.

183

Part 2: How to Keep Your App Updated Across All Platforms

Keeping your cross-platform app updated is critical for providing a seamless experience and ensuring security and performance improvements. Here are some strategies for maintaining your app's updates across all platforms.

1. Using CI/CD for Automatic Updates

The **CI/CD pipeline** can automate the deployment of updates to your app across platforms. With tools like **GitHub Actions**, **Azure DevOps**, or **Jenkins**, you can automatically push updates to production, ensuring your users always have access to the latest version.

1. **Versioning**: Maintain proper version control and manage dependencies to ensure compatibility between different versions of your app across platforms.
2. **Automated Testing**: Integrate automated tests in your CI/CD pipeline to ensure that updates don't break the app's functionality on different platforms.

2. App Store Updates for Mobile Platforms

For **iOS** and **Android**, updates need to be submitted through their respective app stores. This process can be automated using services like **Fastlane**.

184

- **Fastlane** automates tasks like:
  - Pushing updates to **App Store** or **Google Play**.
  - Managing screenshots, metadata, and provisioning profiles.
  - Automating release notes.

3. Updating Desktop Apps

For **desktop apps**, you can use tools like **Electron** (for JavaScript-based desktop apps) to create auto-updating mechanisms. Alternatively, **Windows Store** and **macOS App Store** handle updates for apps distributed through their respective platforms.

4. In-App Updates for Mobile and Desktop

For mobile apps, you can use **in-app update mechanisms** (e.g., Google Play's in-app updates or Apple's internal update system) to push minor updates without requiring users to visit the app store.

For desktop apps, you can implement an **auto-update feature** that checks for the latest version and installs updates automatically.

Part 3: Real-World Example: Monitoring an App Post-Launch

Let's say you've launched a **cross-platform app** that allows users to track fitness goals. Here's how you would monitor the app post-launch and ensure it continues to perform optimally.

1. Monitor App Performance

- **Datadog** is integrated into the app to track response times, error rates, and throughput.
- **Prometheus and Grafana** are used to collect and visualize metrics related to app usage, such as the number of users per day, active sessions, and server resource utilization.

2. Identify Performance Bottlenecks

- Datadog APM helps you identify slow endpoints (e.g., the GET /user-data API) that may be causing latency issues for users.
- Prometheus shows that certain server nodes are under heavy load, leading to slower response times.

3. Resolve Issues

- **Optimize API Endpoints**: Using the insights from Datadog, you optimize the API by caching frequently requested data and implementing pagination.
- **Scale Infrastructure**: Prometheus metrics indicate high CPU usage on certain nodes. You scale the backend services horizontally by adding more instances to handle the load.

4. Push Updates

- Use your **CI/CD pipeline** to deploy the API optimization to production.
- Push updates to **iOS** and **Android** stores using **Fastlane** to provide an updated version of the app with bug fixes and new features.

Conclusion

In this chapter, we discussed the importance of **monitoring** and **maintaining** cross-platform applications to ensure they perform well post-launch. We covered tools like **Datadog**, **Prometheus**, and **Sentry** for monitoring app health and performance, and explored strategies for keeping your app updated across all platforms. With the right monitoring in place, you can identify issues early, resolve them quickly, and continue to improve your app's performance and user experience over time.

CHAPTER 17

SCALING YOUR APPLICATION FOR GLOBAL REACH

As your application gains more users, especially on a global scale, it's essential to plan for scalability. The performance, availability, and user experience of your app can be significantly impacted by how well you scale your infrastructure. In this chapter, we will discuss how to prepare your app for global distribution, deploy it across multiple regions, handle different languages and cultures, and scale your application to accommodate millions of users.

Part 1: Preparing Your App for Global Distribution

To achieve global reach, your application needs to be built with **scalability**, **flexibility**, and **localization** in mind. The goal is to ensure that your app can handle large numbers of users from various geographical locations while delivering a seamless experience tailored to each region.

1. Cloud Infrastructure for Global Distribution

To serve users worldwide efficiently, you must use cloud infrastructure that supports **multi-region deployment**. Cloud providers like **AWS**, **Azure**, and **Google Cloud** offer services that allow you to deploy applications across multiple regions and scale your infrastructure based on demand.

Key considerations for global distribution:

- **Low Latency**: Deploy your app in multiple regions to ensure that users from different locations have fast access to the app.
- **Scalable Infrastructure**: Use cloud services that allow you to scale resources (compute, storage, networking) up or down based on traffic patterns.
- **High Availability**: Ensure your app remains available even if one region faces an issue. Set up **load balancing** and **failover** between regions.

2. Choosing the Right Cloud Services for Multi-Region Deployment

- **Content Delivery Networks (CDNs)**: Services like **AWS CloudFront**, **Azure CDN**, or **Google Cloud CDN** cache your content at edge locations around the world, improving load times and reducing server load.

- **Global Load Balancing**: Use load balancing solutions like **AWS Route 53**, **Azure Traffic Manager**, or **Google Cloud Load Balancer** to route users to the nearest region, ensuring low latency and distributing traffic evenly across multiple regions.

- **Database Replication**: For applications with heavy data requirements, use **multi-region database replication**. Services like **Amazon RDS**, **Azure SQL Database**, and **Google Cloud Spanner** support geographically distributed databases to ensure data is available across regions.

3. Preparing for Cross-Border Regulations

Before deploying your application globally, it's essential to consider regulations that might affect how data is stored and processed:

- **GDPR**: If you're serving users in the **EU**, ensure that your application complies with **General Data Protection Regulation (GDPR)** by storing data locally within the EU or having clear data processing agreements.

- **Data Residency Laws**: Countries like **China** and **Russia** have strict data residency laws that require data to be stored locally.

4. Localized Services and Regional Considerations

Depending on the region, your application may need to adapt in various ways:

- **Localization and Translation**: Support multiple languages and character sets (e.g., Arabic, Chinese, etc.) to provide a localized user experience.
- **Currency and Payment Methods**: Offer region-specific payment methods and currency formatting (e.g., USD, EUR, JPY).
- **Time Zones and Date Formats**: Ensure that the app handles time zones and formats correctly. For example, **ISO 8601** for date and time formats ensures compatibility across regions.

Part 2: Multi-Region Deployment and Handling Different Languages/Cultures

1. Deploying Across Multiple Regions

As your app scales globally, it is important to deploy it in multiple regions to reduce latency and improve user experience. Here's how to approach multi-region deployment:

1.1 Multi-Region Deployment Strategy:

1. **Global Load Balancing**: Use **DNS-based load balancing** to route users to the nearest data center. This ensures that users always interact with the closest server, reducing latency and improving response times.

2. **Data Replication**: Set up **multi-region database replication** to ensure your data is available globally and remains consistent across regions. Services like **Amazon Aurora Global Databases** or **Azure Cosmos DB** offer seamless multi-region replication.

3. **Automated Scaling**: Use cloud auto-scaling features to automatically scale your app in response to traffic patterns. For example, **AWS Auto Scaling** or **Azure Scale Sets** can automatically add or remove resources based on demand.

1.2 Example of Multi-Region Deployment Using AWS

For a cross-platform app, you could deploy a backend to **AWS** across multiple regions:

1. **AWS Regions**: Deploy your app in multiple regions like **US-East**, **EU-West**, and **Asia-Pacific**.

2. **S3 and CloudFront**: Use **Amazon S3** for global file storage and **AWS CloudFront** for content delivery across the globe.

3. **Route 53**: Use **AWS Route 53** for routing traffic to the nearest AWS region, improving latency for users.

```bash
aws configure set region us-east-1  # Set region
for your instance
aws ec2 create-security-group --group-name my-
security-group --description "My security group"
```

2. Handling Different Languages and Cultures

Localization and internationalization are critical for making your app accessible to a global audience. Here's how to handle multiple languages and cultural preferences:

2.1 Text Translation and Internationalization (i18n)

- **Python**: Use libraries like **Babel** or **gettext** to handle translations and localization in Python applications.
  - Example:

```python
```

```
from babel import Locale
from     babel.support     import
Translations

# Set the locale for Spanish
locale = Locale('es', 'ES')
translations                =
Translations.load('locales',
locale=locale)
print(translations.gettext('Hello,
World!'))
```

- **C#**: Use **Resource Files (.resx)** for storing localized text and automatically switch between languages.
  - Example:

```
csharp
```

```
ResourceManager     rm     =     new
ResourceManager("MyApp.Resources",
Assembly.GetExecutingAssembly());
string          greeting          =
rm.GetString("Greeting",
CultureInfo.CurrentCulture);
Console.WriteLine(greeting);
```

2.2 Handling Cultural Differences

- **Currency Formatting**: Use libraries or built-in functions to format currency according to the user's location (e.g., USD, EUR).
    - **Python**:

    ```python
    from babel import Locale
    from babel.numbers import import
    format_currency

    print(format_currency(1000, 'USD',
    locale='en_US'))         #    Output:
    $1,000.00
    ```

- **Date and Time Formatting**: Different cultures have varying formats for date and time. Ensure the app handles these differences.
    - **Python** (using **Babel**):

    ```python
    from babel import Locale
    from babel.dates import format_date
    from datetime import date
    ```

```
print(format_date(date.today(),
locale='en_US'))  # Output: December
1, 2021
```

- **Payment Methods**: Provide localized payment options depending on the region. For example, support **PayPal**, **Stripe**, and **Alipay** for different markets.

Part 3: Real-World Example: Scaling an Application for Millions of Users

Let's consider a **real-world example** of scaling a cross-platform e-commerce application that serves millions of users across multiple regions.

1. Initial Architecture and Challenges

The e-commerce app starts with basic architecture hosted in a single region. As the user base grows globally, the app faces performance issues such as:

- Slow response times from users located far from the server.
- Increased load during shopping seasons, causing performance bottlenecks.

- Difficulty handling large datasets due to high concurrency from multiple regions.

2. Multi-Region Deployment

To solve these issues:

- The app is deployed across **multiple AWS regions** (e.g., **US-East**, **EU-West**, **Asia-Pacific**).
- **AWS S3** stores product images and **CloudFront** is used for caching content at edge locations, minimizing latency for global users.
- **Amazon Aurora Global Databases** replicates product data across regions, ensuring users get fast access to product information.

3. Load Balancing and Auto-Scaling

- **AWS Route 53** is used to route users to the closest AWS region based on their location.
- **Auto Scaling Groups** dynamically scale the app's compute resources based on traffic volume.

4. Database Optimization

- The app uses **read replicas** to distribute read queries to different regions, reducing the load on the main database and improving response times.

5. Localization and Payment Integration

- The app offers localized content in **English**, **Spanish**, **French**, and **Mandarin**.
- **Currency** is automatically converted based on the user's region, and **local payment methods** (e.g., **Stripe**, **Alipay**) are offered to improve conversion rates.

6. Monitoring and Performance Management

- **Datadog** is used to monitor application performance across regions, tracking response times, error rates, and system health in real-time.
- **Prometheus** and **Grafana** are used to collect performance metrics and visualize server load and resource consumption.

7. Results

- The app's global user base enjoys low-latency access to product data, fast checkout processes, and an improved user experience.
- The app automatically scales during peak shopping periods, ensuring availability even with millions of users.

Conclusion

In this chapter, we discussed how to **prepare** and **scale** a cross-platform application for global distribution. Key strategies for scaling include **multi-region deployment**, **localization** for different languages and cultures, and optimizing for **global infrastructure** using cloud platforms like **AWS** and **Azure**. We also presented a real-world example of scaling an e-commerce app, illustrating the challenges and solutions related to handling millions of users across regions. By following these strategies, you can ensure that your cross-platform app can scale effectively to meet global demand while providing a seamless user experience.

CHAPTER 18

THE FUTURE OF CROSS-PLATFORM DEVELOPMENT

As the demand for seamless, high-performing applications continues to grow, **cross-platform development** is evolving to meet the needs of modern software ecosystems. New technologies, tools, and practices are constantly reshaping how developers build and maintain applications across multiple platforms. This chapter will explore the **future trends in cross-platform development**, examine the **evolving role of DevOps** in building modern apps, and discuss a **forward-looking project** that integrates new tools and practices.

Part 1: Trends in Cross-Platform Development, Including Emerging Technologies

Cross-platform development has come a long way in terms of efficiency, performance, and user experience. As technology continues to advance, several emerging trends are reshaping the landscape of cross-platform app development.

1. Emerging Technologies in Cross-Platform Development

- **WebAssembly (Wasm)**: WebAssembly is gaining traction as a powerful way to run high-performance code in the browser. It allows developers to write cross-platform applications in languages like **C**, **C++**, **Rust**, and **Go**, which can then be compiled to run efficiently in web browsers. WebAssembly is expected to play a significant role in building more performant, portable, and lightweight web applications that work seamlessly across all devices.
    - o **Use Case**: A web app that uses **Rust** to process data in the browser at near-native speed, eliminating the need for native apps.
- **Flutter**: Initially designed for mobile app development, **Flutter** by Google has rapidly expanded its capabilities to support **desktop** and **web** applications as well. Its single codebase for all platforms, combined with powerful performance optimizations, makes it a strong contender for cross-platform development in the future. Additionally, the community-driven growth and continued support from Google make Flutter a popular choice for modern app development.

- o **Use Case**: Building an app that looks and performs consistently across **iOS**, **Android**, **Windows**, **macOS**, and **Linux** with Flutter.

- **Progressive Web Apps (PWAs)**: PWAs are gaining popularity because they provide a native app-like experience on the web. They can work offline, load quickly, and offer push notifications, all while being built using standard web technologies like HTML, CSS, and JavaScript. PWAs are increasingly being adopted as an alternative to native apps, especially for businesses looking to target multiple platforms without maintaining separate native codebases.

  - o **Use Case**: A retail app that behaves like a native mobile app but is built as a PWA, providing a consistent experience across browsers and devices without needing to install an app.

- **Unified Development with JavaScript and TypeScript**: With tools like **React Native**, **Ionic**, and **Electron**, developers are able to leverage **JavaScript** and **TypeScript** to create mobile, web, and desktop applications from a single codebase. This trend is expected to continue as the demand for quicker development cycles and more versatile applications grows.

- o **Use Case**: A **TypeScript-based** app using **React Native** for mobile, **Electron** for desktop, and **React** for the web, ensuring a consistent experience across platforms.

- **Artificial Intelligence and Machine Learning Integration**: AI and ML are becoming integral parts of modern applications. As cross-platform tools become more capable, integrating AI/ML into cross-platform apps is becoming easier. Tools like **TensorFlow Lite** for mobile and **Core ML** for iOS are examples of how AI/ML can be used to create smarter, more intuitive apps.

  - o **Use Case**: A mobile app using **TensorFlow Lite** for real-time image recognition, providing a feature that works seamlessly on both Android and iOS.

2. The Importance of Quantum Computing in the Future of Cross-Platform Development

While still in its infancy, **quantum computing** is poised to revolutionize fields such as cryptography, optimization, and machine learning. The future of cross-platform development may include leveraging quantum computing resources through cloud providers like **IBM Quantum** and **Microsoft**

Azure Quantum, enabling developers to experiment with quantum algorithms in a cross-platform environment.

Part 2: The Evolving Role of DevOps in Building Modern Apps

DevOps plays a central role in modern software development, especially for **cross-platform applications**, where continuous integration, automated testing, and deployment pipelines need to be fine-tuned to work across multiple environments. The role of DevOps is continuously evolving with the adoption of new tools, practices, and automation.

1. The Growth of DevOps Automation

As cross-platform development becomes more complex, automation becomes a key enabler for speeding up delivery cycles and ensuring consistent quality. Here are some significant DevOps trends that will shape the future of app development:

- **Automated Testing Across Platforms**: Testing frameworks and tools like **Selenium**, **Appium**, **Cypress**, and **TestCafe** enable the automation of testing across web and mobile platforms. Continuous testing in CI/CD pipelines ensures that code is tested in various environments before reaching users.

- o **Example**: A mobile app using **Appium** for automated testing across iOS and Android platforms, integrated into the CI/CD pipeline.

- **Infrastructure as Code (IaC)**: Tools like **Terraform** and **AWS CloudFormation** allow developers to define cloud infrastructure as code, making it easier to set up and manage scalable infrastructure across multiple regions and platforms. IaC ensures that environments are reproducible and consistent, which is crucial for cross-platform applications.

  - o **Example**: Using **Terraform** to automatically deploy and configure multi-region cloud infrastructure for a global application.

- **Containerization and Microservices**: The adoption of containers (via **Docker**) and microservices architecture enables teams to build applications in modular, isolated services. These services can be deployed and scaled independently across different platforms, ensuring flexibility and reducing deployment complexity.

- o **Example**: A microservices-based app deployed in containers using **Docker**, orchestrated with **Kubernetes** to scale across global data centers.

- **Continuous Monitoring and Observability**: DevOps increasingly incorporates monitoring and observability practices, allowing teams to track app performance in real time. Tools like **Datadog**, **Prometheus**, **Grafana**, and **New Relic** provide in-depth insights into app health across multiple platforms, enabling developers to quickly identify and address issues.

  - o **Example**: A web app using **Prometheus** to monitor server health and **Grafana** for visualizing system performance across regions.

2. Shift Left in DevOps

The concept of shifting left refers to moving **testing**, **security**, and **quality assurance** earlier in the development cycle, ensuring that issues are caught earlier in the process. This trend is especially important for cross-platform development, where platform-specific bugs might go unnoticed in traditional testing cycles. Integrating security checks, unit tests, and automated code quality checks into the CI/CD pipeline is becoming increasingly common.

- **Example**: A **GitHub Actions** pipeline that runs unit tests, checks for security vulnerabilities, and performs linting for **JavaScript**, **C#**, and **Python** before code is merged into the main branch.

Part 3: Real-World Example: A Forward-Looking Project That Integrates New Tools and Practices

Let's take a forward-looking example of a **cross-platform health and fitness app** that leverages the latest technologies in its development process. This example will show how emerging tools, practices, and automation can be integrated into a project.

1. The Project: Cross-Platform Health and Fitness App

The health app will be built to run on mobile (iOS, Android), desktop (Windows, macOS), and web platforms. The app will use real-time data (e.g., exercise tracking, nutrition data) and leverage AI for personalized recommendations.

2. Technology Stack:

- **Frontend**: Flutter for mobile and web, Electron for desktop
- **Backend**: Node.js with Express.js

- **AI/ML**: TensorFlow Lite for mobile, TensorFlow for backend recommendation engine
- **Database**: MongoDB with multi-region replication for fast global access
- **Cloud**: AWS for hosting, with **Elastic Beanstalk** for deployment
- **CI/CD**: GitHub Actions for automated testing, build, and deployment

3. DevOps Automation:

1. **Automated Testing**: Automated tests for the app's **mobile**, **web**, and **desktop** versions are set up using **Appium** and **Cypress**. Tests are run automatically in the CI pipeline whenever changes are made.

2. **Docker**: The app's backend is containerized using Docker, and **AWS Fargate** is used to deploy containers without managing servers.

3. **Kubernetes**: The app's microservices are orchestrated using **Kubernetes**, allowing for easy scaling and management of different services across cloud regions.

4. **Monitoring**: The app's performance is monitored using **Datadog**, which tracks metrics like API response times, error rates, and infrastructure usage in real time.

5. **Continuous Delivery**: The app is deployed automatically through a **CI/CD pipeline**, ensuring that the latest features and bug fixes are quickly pushed to all platforms.

4. Scaling the App:

- **Multi-Region Deployment**: The backend is deployed in multiple AWS regions to handle traffic from users in North America, Europe, and Asia. AWS **Route 53** is used for global DNS load balancing, ensuring that users are directed to the nearest region.
- **Global Content Delivery**: Static assets (e.g., images, workout videos) are stored in **Amazon S3** and delivered globally via **AWS CloudFront** for low-latency access.
- **Data Replication**: MongoDB is configured for global replication, ensuring that data is available quickly to users across different regions.

5. AI/ML for Personalization:

- The app uses machine learning models to analyze user data and provide personalized exercise plans and nutrition recommendations.
- **TensorFlow Lite** is used on mobile devices to make real-time recommendations based on sensor data (e.g., accelerometer for activity tracking).
- The backend uses **TensorFlow** to process historical data and provide long-term health insights.

Conclusion

In this chapter, we explored the **future of cross-platform development**, focusing on emerging technologies like **WebAssembly, Flutter, Progressive Web Apps (PWAs)**, and the role of **AI/ML** in building smarter applications. We also discussed the evolving role of **DevOps**, from automation to continuous monitoring, and its importance in the modern development lifecycle. Finally, we walked through a **real-world example** of a health app that integrates new tools, practices, and technologies to scale globally, highlighting how emerging tools and DevOps practices can be used to build modern, scalable applications. As cross-platform development continues to evolve, staying up to date with these trends will ensure that your applications remain competitive and meet the needs of a global audience.

www.ingramcontent.com/pod-product-compliance
Lightning Source LLC
LaVergne TN
LVHW022342060326
832902LV00022B/4190